Em

WUTHERING HEIGHTS

E. L. Gilbert
Department of English
Brooklyn College

BARNES & NOBLE
BOOKS
NEW YORK

This edition published by Barnes & Noble, Inc.,
by arrangement with Macmillan Publishing USA,
a division of Simon & Schuster, Inc.

1997 Barnes & Noble Books

Macmillan Publishing USA
A division of Simon & Schuster, Inc.
1633 Broadway
New York, NY 10019

ISBN 0-7607-0835-5

Text design by Tony Meisel

Printed and bound in the United States of America.

97 98 99 00 01 M 9 8 7 6 5 4 3 2 1

RRDC

CONTENTS

INTRODUCTION TO EMILY BRONTË

THE BRONTËS

One cannot speak of Emily Brontë without also speaking of her family, "that family of poets," as Thackeray described them, "in their solitude yonder on the gloomy Northern moors."

After filling a number of minor clerical positions, the Reverend Patrick Brontë, born "Brunty" in County Down, Ireland, became curate of Haworth, a lonely parish set in the wild moors of Yorkshire, England. There he lived with his wife, Maria Branwell, and their six children, Maria, Elizabeth, Charlotte, Patrick Branwell, Emily Jane, and Anne. In 1821, the mother died of cancer, after which the children were raised by their aunt, Elizabeth Branwell, and by a kindly Yorkshire servant, Tabby.

The young Brontës had their lessons to learn, under the guidance of their father, and their household duties to perform, but for the rest, they were thrown back upon themselves for companionship and upon their vivid imaginations for pleasure and excitement. Together they roamed the beautiful, desolate moors, or pored over the volumes in the local lending library. In 1824, the four oldest girls were sent off to a boarding school for clergymen's daughters at Casterton. As a result of the treatment they received there, Maria and Elizabeth died, and Charlotte herself came perilously close to death. She lived, however, to confer a terrible immortality upon the school, describing it in detail under the name of Lowood, in *Jane Eyre*.

In 1826, the Reverend Brontë returned from a trip to Leeds with some toys for his children, never dreaming that this simple, fatherly gesture was to have an enormous impact on the history of English Literature. Among the toys was a set of wooden soldiers. Immediately the children's imaginations created around these toys the history of two rival kingdoms, Angria and Gondal. Charlotte and Branwell became the historians of Angria, and Emily and Anne composed the *Gondal Chronical*, a long and complex account, embellished with verses by Emily, of a mysterious northern kingdom. Most of this material was later to be destroyed, but enough has survived, notably Emily's poetry, to suggest the elaborateness and the seriousness of the project, a project which occupied the Brontës well into their adult lives, and which foreshadowed much that was to appear later in their mature work.

As they grew older, the children spent short periods of time away from Haworth. Emily and Charlotte sought to supplement the family income by becoming teachers, and in 1842 they lived for eight months in Brussels, learning French, German and music. But from these absences Emily, especially, always returned with an overwhelming sense of relief to her beloved moors, to which she felt an almost mystical attachment.

By 1845 the three girls were once more together at Haworth, their aunt having died and the dissolute Branwell rapidly falling under the influence of drink and drugs.

It was at this time that the girls discovered their mutual preoccupation with poetry. Each had been writing in private, but in 1846 they pooled their work and brought out, at their own expense, the volume entitled *Poems by Currer, Ellis and Acton Bell*. The book sold only two copies but its authors were not discouraged. They turned to the writing of fiction, and after many disappointments saw the publication, in 1847, of Charlotte's novel, *Jane Eyre*. The work was well received, and late in the same year Emily's *Wuthering Heights* and Anne's *Agnes Grey* were also published, under the same pseudonyms as had appeared on the book of poems. Critics immediately began to speculate that the novels were all the work of the same author, and Charlotte took the occasion of the second edition of *Wuthering Heights*, in 1850, to lay the facts before the world.

By this time, however, Anne and Emily had both died (in 1848), as Branwell had before them, and Charlotte's *Biographical Notice of Ellis and Acton Bell* took on many of the aspects of a eulogy. Of her sister Emily's last illness, she wrote:

Day by day, when I saw with what a front she met suffering, I looked on her with an anguish of wonder and love. I have seen nothing like it; but, indeed, I have never seen her parallel in anything. Stronger than a man, simpler than a child, her nature stood alone. The awful point was, that, while full of truth for others, on herself she had no pity; the spirit was inexorable to the flesh, from the trembling hand, the unnerved limbs, the faded eyes, the same service was exacted as they had rendered in health.

And of Emily's character, Charlotte produced a paragraph that might well have appeared in *Wuthering Heights*:

> In Emily's nature the extremes of vigour and simplicity seemed to meet. Under an unsophisticated culture, in artificial tastes, and an unpretending outside, lay a secret power and fire that might have informed the brain and kindled the veins of a hero; but she had no worldly wisdom; her powers were unadapted to the practical business of life; she would fail to defend her most manifest rights, to consult her most legitimate advantage. An interpreter ought always to have stood between her and the world. Her will was not very flexible, and it generally opposed her interest. Her temper was magnanimous, but warm and sudden; her spirit altogether unbending.

Emily Brontë was perhaps not so unworldly, not so unadapted to the practical business of life as her sister suggested she was. At any rate, in *Wuthering Heights* she gives evidence of having had a very firm grasp of those realities of life with which she came into contact every day, and beyond that, of those realities whose mastery we might even be surprised to find in the average lawyer. In his essay "The Structure of *Wuthering Heights*," C. P. Sanger marvels at the precision with which Emily handles the passage of time in her novel, the gradual aging of her characters, the intricate family relationships, the topography and the botany of the area, and, perhaps, most surprising, the complex laws of property. Much of the plot of *Wuthering Heights* turns on the rules of inheritance of the day, and Emily's understanding of these rules seems to have been all that the most practical person could desire.

WUTHERING HEIGHTS BACKGROUND

WUTHERING HEIGHTS

Still, it would clearly be wrong to speak of *Wuthering Heights* as a worldly book. The chief qualities of Emily Brontë's mind, as they emerge from the story, are its lyrical bent and its mysticism. By mid–nineteenth-century standards, *Wuthering Heights* is indeed the rude, insular book a number of its first critics found it. For where such authors as Jane Austen, George Eliot, Thackeray, and Trollope were representing people's chief struggle as essentially a social one, Emily Brontë saw the principal human conflict as one between the individual and the dark, questioning universe, a universe symbolized, in her novel, both by the threatening and hardly-to-be-controlled inner nature of humans, and by nature in its more impersonal sense, the wild, lonesome mystery of the moors.

Thus the love of Heathcliff and Catherine, in its purest form, expresses itself absolutely in its own terms. These terms may seem, to a conventional mind, violent, and even repellent. But having been generated by that particular love, they are the proper expressions of it. The passionately private relationship of Heathcliff and Catherine makes no reference to any social convention or situation, and, indeed, it is doomed only when Cathy begins to be attracted to the genteel ways and the social graces of Thrushcross Grange, and is led, through them, to abandon her true nature. Whether or not we try to account for this extraordinary inwardness of Emily Brontë's book by noting the author's gloomy, isolated childhood, that inwardness, that remarkable sense of the privacy of human experience, is clearly the central vision of *Wuthering Heights*.

Inwardness is also the key to the structure of the novel. The book begins in the year 1801, on the very rim of the tale, long after the principal incidents of the story have taken place. We are far, then, from the heart of the novel in the first pages, and our guide, Mr. Lockwood, is also, like us, very far removed from the central experience of the narrative. We blunder along, under Lockwood's sadly unperceptive direction, and only very slowly do we begin to understand, in spite of, rather than because of, our guide's help, what it is that has happened at Wuthering Heights and Thrushcross Grange. Gradually we spiral in toward the center. In a few chapters, Nelly Dean, a person who has actually participated in the story, takes over from Lockwood, and we are a little closer to the truth. Still Nelly is herself unperceptive, and we must struggle hard before we can actually achieve the true center of the novel, the passionate last meeting of Heathcliff and Cathy in chapter 15, in which, for a moment, we are permitted to stare into the heart of the fiery furnace.

HEATHCLIFF AND THE SATANIC HERO

Such inwardness, both of content and of structure, is particularly characteristic of writers from the Romantic Period. And as such writers came more and more to concentrate in their work on man's inner nature, they came more and more to discover the hard core of darkness and violence in every human being. Thus there began to appear, in the late eighteenth and the early nineteenth century, a new kind of hero, the so-called Satanic hero, a figure of strength and creativity, like older heroes, but now a creature of darkness and rebellious passion as well.

For example, it was during the early nineteenth century that there first began to appear, in literary criticism, the idea that Satan, and not God, might be the true hero of Milton's *Paradise Lost*. Milton describes Satan in terms that would surely seem appropriate as a description of Heathcliff:

> . . . He, above the rest, In shape and gesture proudly eminent, Stood like a tower. His form had not yet lost All her original brightness, nor appeared Less than Archangel ruined, and the excess Of glory obscured: as when

> the sun new-risen Looks through the horizontal misty air Shorn of his beams, or from behind the moon, In dim eclipse, disastrous twilight sheds On half the nations, and with fear of change Perplexes monarchs. Darkened so, yet shone Above them all the archangel; but his face Deep scars of thunder had entrenched, and care Sat on his faded cheek, but under brows Of dauntless courage, and considerate pride Waiting revenge. Cruel his eye, but cast Signs of remorse and passion, to behold The fellows of his crime, the followers rather (Far other once beheld in bliss), condemned Forever now to have their lot in pain. . . .

Of Milton's *Paradise Lost*, the visionary poet, William Blake, one of the earliest Romantics, said, "The reason Milton wrote in fetters when he wrote of Angels and God, and at liberty when of Devils and Hell, is because he was a true Poet and of the Devil's party without knowing it." And the Romantic leader Shelley wrote, "Milton's Devil, as a moral being, is . . . far superior to his God."

One of the earliest of the Satanic heroes, built in part on the model of Milton's creation, is the character of Father Schedoni in Ann Radcliffe's 1797 novel *The Italian, or The Confessional of the Black Penitents*, a Gothic tale of the kind very popular with the Romantics. Mrs. Radcliffe's description of Schedoni is in the best tradition of the type:

> His was not the melancholy of a sensible and wounded heart, but apparently that of a gloomy and ferocious disposition. There was something in his physiognomy extremely singular, and that cannot easily be defined. It bore the traces of many passions, which seemed to have fixed the features they no longer animated. An habitual gloom and severity prevailed over the deep lines of his countenance; and his eyes were so piercing that they seemed to penetrate, at a single glance, into the hearts

> of men, and to read their most secret thoughts; few persons could support their scrutiny, or even endure to meet them twice.

Emily Brontë's Heathcliff is plainly in the Satanic-Napoleonic-Byronic tradition of Byron's Manfred, Shelley's Prometheus, Pushkin's Eugen Onegin and Melville's Captain Ahab. Indeed, when we compare Heathcliff with Charlotte Brontë's Rochester in *Jane Eyre*, we can appreciate with special intensity how rich and many-layered a creation the former is.

Charlotte's Rochester is, like Heathcliff, a dark, forbidding figure. Yet the reason for his gloominess is essentially external. The past which haunts him every day takes the form of his mad wife. And though that past is a terrible burden, a warping influence on his life, it nevertheless is capable of being removed. Fate can carry that wife away, and with the wife, a large portion of the guilt. Thus Rochester's restoration involves the removal of an external pressure and as such is a comparatively simple matter, just as the story in which he appears strikes readers today as a little superficial and old-fashioned.

The pressures on Heathcliff, on the other hand, are internal. True, they are in part the products of external circumstances—the orphan years in Liverpool, the vicious treatment at Wuthering Heights. But what these events have done is to develop and to exaggerate, Emily Brontë suggests, the darkness and violence that was in Heathcliff from the beginning, as it is in everyone. And because this darkness is so primal and so universal, it can never be overcome. It persists, implacable and unchangeable, a comment not just on one man's special sorrow but on everyone's dark heritage. Heathcliff is a powerful figure not only because he is rooted in the traditions of his own time, from which he draws strength, but also because he makes a universal statement about the nature of being human, which continues to strike readers today as remarkably fresh and modern.

GENEALOGICAL TABLE

Mr. Earnshaw d. Oct. 1777 m. Mrs. Earnshaw d. Spring 1773

Mr. Linton d. Autumn 1780 m. Mrs. Linton d. Autumn 1780

Hindley b. Summer 1757 d. Sept. m. 1777 Frances b. d. late 1778

Catherine b. Summer 1765 d. March 20 m. April 1783 Edgar b. 1762 d. Sept. 1801

Heathcliff b. 1764 d. May 1802 m. Jan. 1784 Isabelle b. late 1765 d. June, 1797

Hareton b. June 1778 m. Jan. 1, 1803

Catherine b. Mar. 20, 1784 m. August 1801

Linton b. Sept., 1784 d. Oct, 1801

DETAILED ANALYSIS

When Mr. Lockwood, a new tenant at Thrushcross Grange, goes to pay his first call on his landlord, he finds himself badly treated by the dogs, the servants, and the landlord himself, Mr. Heathcliff. Heathcliff seems a strangely paradoxical figure. Dark-skinned and brooding like a gypsy, he nevertheless exhibits the dress and manners of a country squire. He is as handsome and erect in form as he is gloomy and reserved in behavior.

The name of the landlord's house is Wuthering Heights, a strongly built but battered old farmhouse, its name "descriptive of the atmospheric tumult to which its exposed position subjected it in stormy weather."

Lockwood, his interest aroused in the curious inmates of the Heights, visits again the next day and this time is snowed in and is forced to stay the night despite Heathcliff's obvious displeasure. In the course of his stay he meets the other members of the household: Heathcliff's widowed daughter-in-law, young and pretty but her every glance full of scorn and hatred, and a clumsy young man whose name—Hareton Earnshaw—is to be found carved over the door of Wuthering Heights along with the date "1500."

When it is time for bed, Lockwood is led to a disused bedroom where he finds, scratched in the panelling of a large, enclosed window seat, the names "Catherine Earnshaw," "Catherine Heathcliff," and "Catherine Linton." Idly, the guest turns over the pages of some old books stored in the window seat and discovers diary-like entries on the blank pages. These entries, dated some twenty-five years before and written in the hand of the girl Catherine, tell of her brother Hindley's mistreatment of Heathcliff, of threats to drive Heathcliff away, and of plans that Catherine and Heathcliff have made to rebel against Hindley's tyranny.

Nodding over these old records, Lockwood falls asleep and dreams that a miserable young girl is wailing at the window, tapping on it and begging to be let in after twenty years of wandering. Awaking with a scream and telling his dream to his landlord, Lockwood finds himself thrust aside by the almost maddened Heathcliff, who leans far out into the storm and passionately calls upon the now-invisible Cathy to come in.

Back at Thrushcross Grange, Mr. Lockwood, who has fallen ill in the storm, asks his housekeeper Nelly Dean, long a servant both at the Heights and the Grange, to tell him the story of the strange people he has met. Nelly explains that old Mr. Earnshaw—Hareton's grandfather and Catherine's and Hindley's father—had returned from a trip to Liverpool one day with a dark little boy he had found abandoned there. He had named the boy Heathcliff and was as pleased with the child's silent toughness as he was displeased with his own son's weakness. Catherine was happy to have a new companion, but from the first Hindley hated the child who, he thought, had supplanted him in his father's affection.

With the death of old Earnshaw, Hindley came into possession of Wuthering Heights and began his long career as tormentor of Heathcliff. He treated him like a servant and tried to keep him from his sister, but Cathy and Heathcliff swore to stay together and grow up like savages on the moors.

During one excursion on the moors, the two approach the refined and beautifully appointed Thrushcross Grange, home of the Lintons, and Catherine, having been bitten by a watchdog, is taken in and kept recuperating for five weeks. It is in these weeks that Catherine becomes acquainted with the Linton children, Isabella and Edgar, and begins to develop a taste for the life of gentility at the Grange. Heathcliff is driven off by the Lintons as if he were an animal.

Not long after this, Hindley's wife dies while giving birth to Hareton, and Hindley, distracted by his loss, turns for solace to drink, and to his favorite sport, the tormenting of Heathcliff. Thus, while Cathy flowers into a beautiful, willful young woman, Heathcliff sinks deeper and deeper into sullen savagery.

One day Catherine tells Nelly Dean that Edgar Linton has proposed to her and that she has decided to accept him. She has made the decision reluctantly, knowing that the refined, placid Edgar is as unlike her as possible, and knowing, too, that the poor, degraded Heathcliff is "more myself than I am." Still, though she feels that what she is about to do is wrong, she rejects Heathcliff as socially beneath her, and consents to marry Edgar.

Heathcliff overhears this conversation and vanishes from Wuthering Heights. Catherine and Nelly search the moors all night for him in vain, and the next day Catherine falls ill with a dangerous fever, from which she only slowly recovers. As it is, three years are to pass without a word from Heathcliff before Catherine permits her marriage to Edgar to take place.

After the marriage Heathcliff reappears, well-dressed, handsome and with plenty of money, the source of which we are never told. Catherine is a good deal more delighted to see him than Edgar is, and strangely enough, Hindley is happy to take him on as a paying guest at the Heights. Hindley, given over entirely to dissipation now, begins to gamble with Heathcliff and very soon falls deeply into debt to the man he very slowly comes to realize is his worst enemy.

Meanwhile, Heathcliff makes frequent visits to the Grange to see Catherine and when, on one occasion, he is ordered from the place by Edgar, who threatens physical violence, he takes his revenge by eloping with Linton's sister, Isabella, who has become infatuated with him. Now, if Edgar should die without a male heir, all of Thrushcross Grange will pass, through Isabella, into the hands of Heathcliff.

Isabella soon comes to see that she has married a devil. She begs Nelly Dean to visit her, and when the housekeeper appears at Wuthering Heights, Heathcliff takes advantage of the visit to arrange a meeting with Catherine, who has been ailing ever since the quarrel between the two men.

The moment Heathcliff sees Catherine he knows that she is dying. Distracted, he accuses her of having killed him and herself by betraying her true nature and her real love. When, later that night, the girl dies, having given birth to a daughter, also named Catherine, Heathcliff beats his head against a tree in his agony, calling upon his dead love to haunt him always.

Soon afterward, Isabella escapes to London, where Heathcliff's sickly son, Linton, is born, and where she dies a dozen years later. Linton is brought to Thrushcross Grange just as Hindley Earnshaw dies, having mortgaged all his property to Heathcliff. Thus, the moment for Heathcliff's revenge now seems at hand. His plan is to destroy the Earnshaws and to unite the properties of the Heights and the Grange, and for this purpose he has kept Hindley's son Hareton an ignorant savage and has forced his own weak, whining son, Linton, into a marriage with the young Cathy. So it is that when Edgar dies, followed soon by Linton—who has been led to bequeath all his property to his father—Heathcliff comes into possession of the whole corner of the world from which, as a boy, he had been so heartlessly driven.

With this revelation, Nelly Dean's narrative comes to an end, and it is left to Lockwood to discover for himself the dramatic conclusion of the story. He leaves the Grange for some time and on his return finds that Heathcliff has died. Catherine Linton, he learns, has won the love of the raw but basically decent Hareton, and Heathcliff, more and more preoccupied with his desire to rejoin Catherine, no longer possessed the diabolical energy with which, in the past, he might have tormented the young lovers. Toward the end he had even stopped eating, and one day he was found dead in the very window seat in which Lockwood had first heard the cries of the lonely waif at the window.

CHAPTER 1

The date at the beginning of the novel is 1801. In this year, Mr. Lockwood, a fashionable gentleman, rents a house in a lonely and desolate corner of northern England owned by a Mr. Heathcliff. Wuthering Heights, written in the form of Lockwood's diary, is the story of Heathcliff, and of his two houses—Thrushcross Grange, which Linton rents, and Wuthering Heights, where he himself resides.

The desolation of this northern landscape suits Lockwood perfectly, for he likes to think of himself as proud and antisocial. Indeed, he is soon telling us of a recent trip he took to the seaside where, having found himself falling in love with a young woman who seemed silently to be returning his affection, he coldly rejected the girl's shy advances and thus earned a reputation for heartlessness.

As soon as he gets a chance, Lockwood goes to pay a call on Heathcliff at nearby Wuthering Heights. A fierce "Walk in!" through closed teeth is Heathcliff's only invitation to his new tenant, and as Joseph, an ancient servant, leads Lockwood's horse away, the two men enter the rustic wood and stone building, which is covered with grotesque carvings and marked over the door with the date "1500" and the name Hareton Earnshaw.

Once inside the house Lockwood is left alone by his host, who goes down to the cellar for wine. To pass the time, the visitor tries to be friendly with Heathcliff's dogs, but the animals are not kept for pets. Like their master, they have been trained to be vicious, and at Lockwood's first gesture, they attack. A "lusty dame" from the kitchen, whose name we later learn is Zillah, hurries in to call the beasts off, and Heathcliff's sole remark to Lockwood about the dogs is a bad-tempered "they won't meddle with persons who touch nothing."

Only Lockwood's spirited reply—he comments that if he had been bitten, he would have set his signet (that is, his fist) on the biter—relaxes Heathcliff into a show of hospitality. But the friendliness (which Lockwood absurdly attributes to his host's desire not to offend a good tenant) is only momentary. When the visit comes to an end, the guest is aware that his landlord wants to see no more of him. Yet he has found Heathcliff intelligent in conversation and he plans to return, at least in part because he feels so sociable compared with the owner of Wuthering Heights.

COMMENT

Lockwood is the sort of shallow, self-important man who likes to play at being melancholy and misanthropic. (Perhaps he has picked up this affectation from the popular fiction of the day, full of brooding, mysteriously unhappy heroes. The so-called Gothic novel, all the rage in Romantic and early-Victorian England, from about 1780–1850, dealt especially with such tortured characters.) He even goes so far as to suggest that the only difference between himself and his gloomy landlord Heathcliff is one of degree. But where Lockwood's melancholy is superficial, Heathcliff's dark and angry vision of life is part of his deepest nature.

"Wuthering," we are told, is a local word "descriptive of the atmospheric tumult"—the wild winds—to which the house is exposed in stormy weather. The continuous battering by the winds has stunted the trees around Wuthering Heights, and the house itself has survived only because it is built of rugged stones and huge, rough, wooden beams. Later in the story we will come to see that the description of the Heights is also a description of its owner. Heathcliff, pictured as dark-skinned, morose, and rather slovenly (but having the manners and dress of a gentleman), has also been twisted and stunted by the storms he has had to endure in his life, and he, too, has survived only because of the brutal strength of character suggested by his name.

Emily Brontë has written a novel which seeks to move ever closer to the center of a unique and remarkable human relationship, and the very structure of her book emphasizes that movement. In Chapter 1, for example, we are as far as possible from the heart of the novel's great experience.

1. The date is 1801, years after the central events of the story.

2. The narrator or diarist, Mr. Lockwood, is a complete stranger to the countryside and to the people, and in his first visit to Wuthering Heights (which is, of course, the reader's first visit too), this superficial man sees only the surface of things.

a. The stunted trees on the Heights have no symbolic meaning for him.

b. The date "1500" and the name Hareton Earnshaw have no special significance.

c. Even Heathcliff seems just another antisocial man.

Later chapters will move progressively closer to the heart of the story, and as they do, this early episode, with its subtle suggestions of an old tragedy and with Lockwood's naïve judgments of Heathcliff, will come to seem prophetic.

CHAPTER 2

Misty, cold weather almost persuades Lockwood to postpone his second trip to Wuthering Heights. But a servant girl has put out the fire in his room, and so he takes his hat and reaches Heathcliff's garden gate just as a snowstorm begins. Running up the flagged path, the visitor finds the door locked and barred (though it is still daytime), and his furious knocking only succeeds in arousing the dour Joseph. The old man announces, in a thick, north country dialect, that not all the knocking in the world will convince either himself or the "missis" within to admit Lockwood, and he leaves the poor man to shiver in the now driving snow.

At this moment a young man with a pitchfork appears and leads Lockwood through a washhouse to the huge, warm room where the tenant had first met with Heathcliff. The "missis," a sullen-looking young woman, is there, but she remains silent, not even offering the guest a seat. Lockwood tries to make polite conversation, but she constantly rebuffs him in a bad-tempered way. As she is about to make tea, she even pauses to ask if Lockwood is an invited guest and, learning that he is not, flings the tea back into the canister. Nevertheless, the girl strikes the visitor as very beautiful, with an admirable figure, an exquisite little face and eyes which, he tells us, were it not for their disagreeable expression, would be irresistible.

The young man with the pitchfork also stares rudely at Lockwood; he is marked by the roughness and lack of cultivation of a laborer, but his bearing is almost haughty and has none of the servility associated with a domestic. Heathcliff enters with a nasty comment about people foolish enough to wander about on the moors in the thick of a snowstorm, and a brusque refusal to lend his visitor a guide back to Thrushcross

Grange. In addition, he orders the girl about so savagely that Lockwood now judges his host to have a genuinely bad nature. Still he tries to be amiable and immediately blunders by referring to the girl as Heathcliff's wife. Heathcliff utters some wild, contemptuous words about his wife being a ministering angel, guarding the fortunes of Wuthering Heights, and Lockwood makes a second error by assuming now that the girl is married to the rough young man. From this whole unlucky conversation certain facts emerge: that the girl is Heathcliff's daughter-in-law, that her husband—Heathcliff's son—is dead, and that the rough young man is named—he makes the announcement himself with great dignity—Hareton Earnshaw.

Lockwood asks several times, with rising irritation, for a guide across the snowy moors, but he is conspicuously ignored by everyone. Joseph enters, muttering viciously about how the young mother will be sure to go right to the devil like her mother before her, and because, in reply, the girl threatens the old man with black magic, Lockwood assumes that she must have some sense of humor and so approaches her for help in his predicament. She offers no help, however, and Lockwood concludes that, there being no one in the house to act as a guide, he must remain the night with neither the young woman nor Heathcliff offering any hospitality.

Furious, Lockwood dashes out of the house, and while Heathcliff, Earnshaw, and the girl argue about whether or not to help him, the guest picks up a lantern and, shouting that he will return it next day, makes for the gate. Joseph reacts automatically. Seeing what appears to him to be a clear case of theft, he sets the dogs on Lockwood; and the visitor, sprawled on the ground and bleeding from the nose, becomes a source of great momentary amusement for Heathcliff. Only the stout housewife Zillah, of all the people at Wuthering Heights, reacts compassionately to Lockwood's plight. She splashes his face with water, gives him a glass of brandy at her master's direction, and finally leads him to a bed.

COMMENT

Chapter 2, while preserving the image of Lockwood as a foolish, conventional, and unperceptive person (he mistakes dead rabbits for household pets just as enthusiastically as he mistakes the young woman first for Heathcliff's wife and then for Earnshaw's), contains a great deal of information about the inhabitants of Wuthering Heights. We learn that Heathcliff had a son, now dead, that the girl was the son's wife, and that there was once a woman in Heathcliff's past of whom he can now speak, however, ironically, as a ministering angel. In addition, the young man's defiant announcement of his name—Hareton Earnshaw—reminds us (though not Lockwood) of the name cut into the doorway of Wuthering Heights, and begins to suggest the complexity of relationships that are to characterize the novel. Most important, the chapter dramatizes the barely suppressed fury and hatred that is the chief element in the atmosphere of Wuthering Heights. Lockwood may be a fool but he hardly deserves the treatment that he gets. The rudeness and inhumanity that were especially associated with Heathcliff in the first chapter, are here shown to have crippled the whole establishment. The girl's beauty is blighted by it; the young man's natural dignity seems to have been debased by association with the house and its owner. Even the viciousness of the dogs appears to be a product of association with the master of Wuthering Heights.

CHAPTER 3

On the way upstairs, Zillah explains that the room she is taking Lockwood to is one which Heathcliff never willingly lets anyone occupy. As a comparatively new member of the household, the kitchen woman cannot explain this strange prohibition, but she cautions silence and then leaves the reluctant guest alone. The bed or couch, Lockwood discovers, is in a little room-within-a-room, so constructed that the ledge of the window, enclosed in the inner chamber, serves as a table. He also notes that certain names have been scratched in the paint of this ledge over and over again, varying from "Catherine Earnshaw" to "Catherine Heathcliff" to "Catherine Linton." Lockwood nods over these names and seems about to dream when he is awakened by the smell of his candle burning the cover of one of the books in the room. Idly, he glances through these volumes, all of which are inscribed "Catherine Earnshaw—her book," with a date a quarter century back and all of whose blank pages are filled with a kind of diary kept by the former owner. His interest aroused now, Lockwood begins to read.

In one entry, Catherine bemoans the death of her father and his replacement by her brother, the tyrannical Hindley, as master of Wuthering Heights. While Hindley and his wife Frances dally in the warm family room one cold and rainy Sunday, Joseph preaches a three-hour sermon in the garret to a shivering Catherine and Heathcliff, afterward forcing some dull, pious texts on them, and when the two young people throw the books away, informing Hindley of their disobedience. Hindley announces that his father had been too kind to Heathcliff, that the boy is a vagabond unfit to eat at the table with the rest of the family and that Catherine must not continue to play with him, on pain of his being sent away. Heathcliff must be reduced, Hindley swears, to his right place.

Lockwood wants to continue reading, but his exertions and the brandy now take effect. He falls asleep and almost immediately begins to dream that it is morning and that he is on his way home with Joseph for a guide. He is, however, accused by the old man of some unnamed sin which he must expiate before he is allowed to return home, and is led to a nearby chapel to suffer through an endless sermon. Lockwood rises to protest but is shouted down by the preacher and is attacked with clubs by the whole congregation, especially Joseph. Fortunately, the dreamer awakens at just this moment to find that the knocking together of clubs in his nightmare is merely the rattling of dry fir-tree cones against his window in the storm.

He now falls asleep again and has a second dream, more disturbing than the first. This time he is within the little chamber when the tapping on the window again disturbs him. Finding the latch soldered closed, he breaks a pane and reaches his hand out to snap off the branch, but instead, his fingers close on the fingers of a little, ice-cold hand, and a melancholy voice sobs "Let me in—let me in!" A child's face appears at the window and gives its name as Catherine Linton, and when Lockwood discovers that he cannot struggle free of the hand, he pulls the slender wrist onto the broken pane, rubs it back and forth till the blood comes and, to the sound of the pitiful voice crying "Twenty years, I've been a waif for twenty years," awakens screaming.

The scream brings Heathcliff, who approaches the chamber cautiously, asking if anyone is within. When Lockwood replies, the host's fear and astonishment turn to rage that anyone should have shown the guest to this bed. He listens with growing emotion to Lockwood's recital of his dream, sends the visitor out of the room, and then, thinking that he is alone, wrenches open the window and sobs, in an uncontrollable passion of tears, "Come in! Come in! Cathy, do come. Oh do—once more! Oh! My heart's darling! hear me this time—Catherine, at last!"

Lockwood dismisses his host's behavior as superstition and goes below. There, as the household begins to stir, he witnesses more scenes of domestic misery. Hareton Earnshaw mutters curses, Zillah suffers her employer's anger, and the girl defies the furious Heathcliff, who tries to hit her. The unhappy guest is delighted to be able to escape from Wuthering Heights before breakfast and, escorted to the gate of Thrushcross Grange by his host, he struggles the two miles to the house alone and arrives there chilled and exhausted.

COMMENT

The three names, "Catherine Earnshaw," "Catherine Heathcliff," and "Catherine Linton," which Lockwood finds scratched on the window ledge, sum up the whole story of *Wuthering Heights* and suggest again how complex the relationships in the book will be. We can still only guess at the nature of these relationships, for Lockwood is not a particularly intelligent or sympathetic observer, but the very fact that his discoveries are not colored with his own imagination makes them more useful to us. The diary entry, for example, gives us a frightening glimpse into the kind of life the young Heathcliff had to live, and helps us to understand the Heathcliff of twenty-five years later. The dream, which at first seems to introduce elements of the supernatural, is psychologically very sound and realistic. The first part of it is pieced together from Lockwood's experiences with Joseph and the household, and his reading of Catherine's books. In the second part, the mournful wraith of Catherine Linton is clearly based on Heathcliff's earlier remark about the ministering angel who guards the fortunes of Wuthering Heights. Only the choice of the name Catherine Linton seems inexplicable in logical terms.

As for Heathcliff's call into the night for Catherine, even Lockwood can sense its terrible, grief-stricken intensity. This is one of the great moments of the novel. Heathcliff, who has all along been presented to us as a vicious man, even as a man of genuine bad nature, is here revealed, for the first time, as a person capable of enormous tenderness and humanity. His whole character deepens and expands at this moment and we are brought one step closer to the central mystery of the book.

Nowhere is Emily Brontë a more remarkable technician than in this chapter, which contains a half dozen separate matters beautifully organized into a single unit. The transitions are especially brilliant. First, Lockwood's drowsing over the names on the ledge prepares us for the dreams to come. Then, the visitor is brought to himself by his candle scorching a calf-skin binding, and this accident draws his and our attention to the books in the little room. The material in the books, itself extremely significant, in turn provides the matter of the first dream, and the end of this dream, with the fir cones tapping at the window, coincides with the beginning of the second dream.

CHAPTER 4

Lockwood manages to spend a few hours in his room, recovering from his ordeal and pretending to enjoy the solitude he has deliberately chosen for himself; but at dusk, when Mrs. Ellen Dean, the housekeeper at Thrushcross Grange, brings him some food, he asks her to stay and encourages her to talk of herself and of her experiences in the neighborhood. This she does freely, and among other things we learn that she has been at the Grange for eighteen years, that times have greatly changed during her stay, that Heathcliff, of whose birth and parentage she knows nothing, is a very wealthy but a very miserly man, and that the young woman at the Heights, Heathcliff's daughter-in-law, was born Catherine Linton, daughter of the late master of Thrushcross Grange. Mrs. Dean also mentions Hareton Earnshaw's relationship to Catherine (for which see the Genealogical Table), his association with Wuthering Heights, where his name appears carved over the door, and the fact that he has been cast out of his inheritance by Heathcliff and is the only person in the parish who does not guess how he has been cheated.

Such facts only whet Lockwood's appetite for information. He encourages Mrs. Dean to tell him as much as she knows about the history of these strange people; the woman agrees, and the reader is now in the hands of a new narrator.

Mrs. Dean tells of how, years before, she had been a servant at Wuthering Heights when old Mr. Earnshaw was master there, and had taken care of his two children, Hindley, fourteen, and Catherine, six. One day, Earnshaw had returned from a trip to Liverpool with a little, dark-skinned, foreign-speaking gypsy boy whom he had found abandoned there and whose plight had touched him. The reaction of everyone in the house to the dirty little creature is disgust. Mrs. Earnshaw wants him removed, the children refuse to have the boy sleep with them, and the young Ellen leaves him out on the landing for the night, hoping he will be gone in the morning.

But Mr. Earnshaw's compassion protects the little orphan—named Heathcliff, after a son who had died at birth—and with the passage of years the gypsy's quiet, if somewhat sullen, behavior earns him a place at the Heights. Mrs. Earnshaw dies, Cathy becomes a good friend of his, and even Mrs. Dean learns a kind of affection for the boy. Only Hindley continues to hate the intruder, feeling that Heathcliff has replaced him in his father's affection. Heathcliff, for his part, learns to take advantage of the coolness that has grown up between Earnshaw and his son over him.

Hindley regularly beats the younger boy, against the express orders of his father, and so whenever Heathcliff wants something—when, for example, his own pony goes lame and he wishes to get Hindley's—he threatens to go to the father with stories of his son's brutalities and of his promise to drive Heathcliff out after old Earnshaw's death; and in this way he triumphs again and again over the embittered heir to Wuthering Heights.

COMMENT

With the appearance of Ellen Dean, who actually participated in many of the most important events of this history, we move still closer to the heart of the novel and to the central relationship of Cathy and Heathcliff.

There are a number of prophetic touches in this chapter. Heathcliff's arrival at the Heights deprives Hindley and Cathy of the gifts their father had promised them, just as his continued presence there is to deprive Hindley of his father's love. And Heathcliff's threat to inform Earnshaw that his son had promised to drive his rival away foreshadows only too accurately what Hindley will in fact do the moment he gets the chance. Hindley's cruelty and cowardice, Catherine's mischievousness and waywardness, and Heathcliff's sullen patience and his enormous potential for vindictiveness, not at first apparent to Ellen Dean, all predict the future.

CHAPTER 5

As time passes, Mr. Earnshaw begins to fail, and as he does so, grows more and more irritable on the subject of Heathcliff. He seems to think that because he likes the boy, everyone else hates him, and in order to humor the old man, as he sits day after day in the chimney corner, the kinder members of the household take to spoiling Heathcliff—no advantage to the boy and his black tempers—and in the process, of course, angering Hindley still more. Finally, on the advice of the local curate, the son is sent to college, though his father believes that he will never thrive anywhere, and the household settles down tolerably, except for the problems created by Joseph and Cathy.

Joseph is described as "the wearisomest, self-righteous Pharisee that ever ransacked a Bible to rake the promises to himself, and fling the curses on his neighbors,"—and Cathy is shown to be a high-spirited, mischievous child, "a wild, wicked slip," who means no harm but who is always plaguing her humorless father with her naughtiness. She is very fond of Heathcliff—indeed, the greatest punishment she can imagine is being separated from him—and often old Earnshaw is angered by the fact that while the child he saved from the streets will obey him only when obedience suits him, he will do Cathy's bidding in anything, even when her orders are couched in what the old man fails to see are only mock-insolent terms. "Nay Cathy," the father says night after night, "I cannot love thee," slowly hardening the girl against him and confirming her in her waywardness. Finally the hour of his death comes. Cathy, subdued a little by illness, is sitting by his knees singing to him as he strokes her hair, Joseph is reading prayers, and Ellen—or Nelly—is knitting. When the death is discovered, Cathy and Heathcliff begin to wail pitifully, and later that night Ellen finds them comforting each other with stories that picture heaven more beautifully than any parson in the world could do.

COMMENT

Chapter 5 offers Nelly Dean's judgment of Joseph and her picture of the lovely, mischievous Cathy, passionate in her attachments, but fond of teasing and tormenting the very people she loves best. The chapter also contains one of the turning points of the book, the death of Mr. Earnshaw. Readers need only recall the excerpt from Cathy's diary in Chapter 3 to know what life is henceforth to be like at Wuthering Heights under the rule of Hindley. It is noteworthy, however, that the chapter ends with a picture of Heathcliff and Cathy comforting each other on the death of Mr. Earnshaw. At this point in the story, there is still, for Heathcliff, a possibility of salvation.

CHAPTER 6

Hindley returns home for the funeral of his father, amazing everyone by bringing with him a wife. Frances is a bright-eyed, slender girl (of no particular name or fortune), whose nearly hysterical reaction to the funeral preparations and pathological terror of dying suggest a high-strung, nervous person. To Ellen she is a young and fresh-complexioned woman, very little likely to die. Nevertheless, her breath comes quick when she mounts the stairs and she has a troublesome cough.

Hindley has grown sparer and lost his color during his three-year absence, and he seems now even colder and more distant than ever as he orders Nelly and Joseph to quarter themselves in the back kitchen. Frances, pleased at first to have found a sister in Catherine, soon tires of the relationship, and as she grows peevish, Hindley grows tyrannical. A few sour words from her about Heathcliff, and all Hindley's hatred is rekindled. He sends the boy to live with the servants, deprives him of the instructions of the curate, and forces him to labor outdoors with the farm hands. Furthermore, he is constantly punishing him and Cathy for their mischievousness and for minor infractions of household rules.

One Sunday evening, having been banished from the sitting-room for making a noise, Heathcliff and Cathy run off to the moors together—one of their pastimes guaranteed to arouse the new master's anger, and Hindley, in a rage, orders the house barred to them for that night. Quite late, when all are in bed, Nelly hears footsteps and hurries downstairs to discover that Heathcliff has returned alone, saying that Cathy will remain behind at Thrushcross Grange. The boy explains what has happened.

He and Cathy had raced across the moors together, he says, to get a glimpse of the people in the Grange. Mr. and Mrs. Linton were not visible, and what the two children saw through the window of the splendidly carpeted, furnished and lighted drawing-room were eleven-year-old Isabella Linton and her fourteen year-old brother Edgar screaming and weeping over who was to get to fondle the family lap dog. Heathcliff's contempt for these two is enormous, and he tacitly speaks for Cathy as well as for himself when he cries, "I'd not exchange, for a thousand lives, my condition here, for Edgar Linton's at Thrushcross Grange—not if I might have the privilege of flinging Joseph off the highest gable, and painting the housefront with Hindley's blood."

Nelly still wants to know why Cathy has remained behind, and Heathcliff continues his story. Their attempts—his and Cathy's—to frighten the Linton children, he explains, roused the house, and as they sought to escape a dog seized Cathy by the ankle. "She did not yell out—no! She would have scorned to do it," Heathcliff announces proudly. "She was sick—not from fear, I'm certain, but from pain." Cathy was carried into the house, followed by the furiously cursing Heathcliff, and when she was recognized, her wound was treated. For Heathcliff, however, there was nothing but scorn from all the Lintons. The boy tells of how he was turned out of the house, of how he waited for a while near the window in case Cathy should need him, of how the beauty and vitality of the girl lighted up all the admiring faces around her, and of how, outcast, he turned reluctantly homeward. "There will be more come of this business than you reckon on," Nelly predicts, and she is right. Heathcliff does not receive a flogging, but he is warned that if he ever speaks to Catherine again he will be dismissed from the Earnshaw household for good.

COMMENT

Chapter 6 is full of foreshadowings. At the outset we are hardly introduced to Frances Linton before we are being prepared for her early death. It is plain that her chief function in the plot is to be as the mother of Hareton. Then, Heathcliff's passionate affirmation of his own and what he believes to be Cathy's values in the face of the pale, weaker-willed Lintons readies us for the tragedy to come. Most important, contact is made for the first time between Wuthering Heights and Thrushcross Grange, and the picture we get of Cathy, seemingly at home after only a few minutes in the beautiful drawing room, and of the swarthy Heathcliff, skulking about the grounds, seeking to protect but forever an outsider, may be taken as an image of the story's central conflict. Only the reader who has reached the end of the novel can fully appreciate the force of Ellen Dean's remark: "There will be more come of this business than you reckon on." Cathy will marry Edgar, Heathcliff Isabella, and the revenge theme, which is so important in the plot, has already begun to take shape.

CHAPTER 7

Cathy remains at Thrushcross Grange for five weeks, and at Christmas returns to the Heights, her ankle thoroughly cured and her manners much improved. She is now fashionably dressed and she enters the house with dignity. She is no longer, in Mrs. Dean's significant phrase, "a wild, hatless little savage . . . rushing to squeeze us all breathless." Readers are left to make their own value judgments of the change. Heathcliff hasn't changed at all, of course, except for having grown more slovenly and neglected in Cathy's absence. Delighted at the boy's dishevelled appearance and at his discomfort, Hindley invites Heathcliff to come forward "like the other servants" and greet the new Catherine. Instead, Heathcliff rushes away, seeing clearly how much the girl has altered in little more than a month with the Lintons.

With the residents of Thrushcross Grange coming to celebrate the holiday next day, preparations begin at Wuthering Heights for the event. Joseph, as might be expected, goes off to pray, and Catherine inspects the gifts that her brother has bought for her to give to the Lintons. Ellen is in the kitchen, getting the holiday meal ready; and, feeling sorry for Heathcliff, she asks the boy to join her. But Heathcliff, gloomy and sullen, prefers to remain out in the stable feeding the animals and caring for a pony.

The young Heathcliff is not, however, the desperate grown man we meet in the first chapters of the novel. There is a basic hopefulness still in his nature at this early stage, and having rushed moodily off to the moors early the next morning, while the others in the household leave for church, he comes back and asks Nelly to help him get cleaned up. The housekeeper is pleased when the boy promises to be better in the future, and she suggests that he ask Cathy's forgiveness for the way he had acted the night before. It is plain that his affection for Cathy and his fear of giving her pain have led him to take this step. As for his feeling that Edgar Linton is better than he is, Nelly reassures the boy, pointing out that young Linton is weak and delicate, while Heathcliff is taller, more powerful and better-looking, and cheering the young man up with charming stories about the royal personages his parents might have been.

These reassurances restore Heathcliff's confidence, and as the Earnshaws and the Lintons return from church, the boy goes out to meet them. Unfortunately, Hindley is the first person to catch sight of Heathcliff, and perhaps irritated at seeing him clean and cheerful, orders him confined to the garret until after the meal. At the same time, Edgar makes an insulting remark about Heathcliff's hair, and infuriated, the boy picks up the first thing that comes to hand—a tureen of hot apple sauce—and dashes it into Edgar's face. In turn, Hindley beats Heathcliff. Cathy, contemptuous of the howling young Lintons, scolds Edgar for having made taunting remarks. Edgar lies to defend himself, insisting that he has said nothing.

The thought that Heathcliff had been beaten and imprisoned powerfully affects Cathy. She does not eat her meal, and during the dancing she slips away to the garret, which she enters by way of a skylight. Nelly follows, to give warning when the time comes when Cathy will be missed; as the girl returns to her guests, Heathcliff, on Cathy's insistence, joins Nelly in the kitchen. There he turns over in his mind schemes for revenge, and when Nelly, shocked, reminds him that vengeance belongs to the Lord, Heathcliff bitterly announces that in this case the Lord is not to have the pleasure!

At this point in her story, Mrs. Dean seeks to break it off. She points out that Mr. Lockwood must be longing for sleep. But

Lockwood says that, on the contrary, he is too absorbed by the tale to sleep, and after praising his housekeeper's story-telling abilities, he settles back to hear more, begging the speaker to omit none of the details.

COMMENT

This chapter is important chiefly for the way in which it gains the reader's sympathy for Heathcliff. The boy's ill usage at Earnshaw's hands, his pathetic attempts to make himself presentable, and the inexcusable contempt he receives from nearly everyone, help to explain his obsessive quest for revenge and to make us accept from him, in the context of the story, what we might reject in another man or a different situation. One of Emily Brontë's most difficult technical challenges was to gain sympathy for a character as destructive as Heathcliff, and Chapter 7 goes far toward solving that problem.

Another technical difficulty the author faced was to explain how so complex and subtle a story, as the one in *Wuthering Heights*, could be told by an ordinary housekeeper. Mr. Lockwood's elaborate praise of Mrs. Dean and the woman's own remarks about her wide reading are an attempt, if perhaps a somewhat contrived one, to confront the issue. It would be just as well, however, not to miss the irony in the scene between Lockwood and his housekeeper. As we shall come to see more and more in the course of the story, Mrs. Dean has not nearly as much intelligence or perceptiveness as her master gives her credit for. In fact, one of the ways in which the author gains sympathy for her protagonist is by forcing the reader into softening some of Nelly's harsher judgments of Heathcliff.

CHAPTER 8

In June, 1778, Hindley's son Hareton Earnshaw is born, and a few months later his mother, weakened by her confinement, dies of consumption. With Frances gone, Hindley grows desperate and gives himself up to reckless dissipation. Of all the servants, only Nelly and Joseph are able to bear the master's evil conduct for long, Nelly because she has been given charge of Hareton, and Joseph because "it was his vocation to be where he had plenty of wickedness to reprove." Hindley's treatment of Heathcliff is enough "to make a fiend of a saint," and in turn, the boy's great delight is to watch Hindley degrading himself.

Wuthering Heights is now an infernal house, Nelly continues. The curate stops calling, and only Edgar Linton's visits to Cathy keep the place in touch with the "decent" world outside. Cathy, at fifteen, has become the neighborhood beauty, though her haughtiness and arrogance alienate even Mrs. Dean. Cathy, however, is wonderfully true to her old attachments, especially to Heathcliff, and young Linton, for all his efforts, cannot make as deep an impression on her as the outcast boy. At this, Mrs. Dean shows Lockwood a portrait of Edgar Linton, the late master of Thrushcross Grange, a rather good likeness which reveals the man's soft-featured refinement but also his want of spirit. Lockwood, for his part, can well understand why Catherine Earnshaw should have chosen this man over Heathcliff for a husband.

Cathy now begins to lead a kind of double life, without actually intending to deceive. At Thrushcross Grange, where she hears Heathcliff referred to as "a vulgar young ruffian," she tries to put into practice all the refinements of behavior she has learned from the Lintons. Home at the Heights, however, she refuses to act with that same politeness that will earn her, instead of praise, only Heathcliff's scorn. She must, of course, suffer for her duplicity whenever Edgar and Heathcliff meet in her presence, and Nelly Dean cannot help but make fun of the social difficulties which the girl's pride makes for her. Still, Cathy frequently comes to confide in the housekeeper as the only soul at the Heights to whom she can turn for advice, and in this way Mrs. Dean gets the sort of intimate information that makes it possible for her to tell her story so well.

One rainy afternoon at the Heights, when Hindley is not at home, Heathcliff gives himself a holiday from the fields and comes to sit with Cathy in the parlor. He has not kept up any curiosity he may once have had about learning, nor maintained even the slightest interest in his appearance, so that both inwardly and outwardly he is "repulsive." Still, he remains pathetically eager for Cathy's companionship and even shows her the almanac in which are marked the number of days the girl has spent with the Lintons and the number she has spent with him.

Cathy is only embarrassed by Heathcliff's appearance in the parlor on this day, however, because she has taken advantage of Hindley's absence to invite Edgar over from the Grange. With young Linton's arrival, Heathcliff slinks out, leaving Catherine to compare his crudity with the sweetness of his rival. Yet Edgar's visit is not to be marked by either sweetness or refinement. Ellen Dean, on orders from Hindley, remains in the parlor with the two young people, and Cathy, who at first quietly urges the housekeeper to go, is soon driven to bad-tempered distraction by her refusal to do so. She pinches the older woman, lies about having done it, slaps her in the face, and when Edgar steps forward to interfere, slaps him too. As far as Mrs. Dean is concerned, it is just as well for Edgar to see the kind of girl Cathy really is, and indeed, young Linton seems on the verge of leaving the Heights, not to return. But at the last moment he has no power to walk out of the house. "He's doomed," says Nelly, "and flies to his fate," for the quarrel has only made the two more intimate and more ready to confess themselves lovers. In the end, Edgar stays at the Heights until Hindley returns later in the day, drunk and dangerous.

COMMENT

This chapter chiefly develops elements in the story that have already been introduced. Hindley's hatred and destructiveness, so long lavished on others, is now, with the death of his wife, turned fully upon himself; and his disintegration will present Heathcliff with an opportunity for revenge. The brutalization of Heathcliff also continues, now apparently unchecked by any of the inner sense of competence and worthiness which had been the boy's in old Earnshaw's time. In addition, Cathy's arrogance and her ambition grow side by side, and her relationship with Edgar Linton, which Heathcliff had so proudly declared an impossibility in Chapter 6, now begins to move inevitably toward marriage.

CHAPTER 9

Hindley's drunken return causes Mrs. Dean to try to hide the infant Hareton in a cupboard. The child is so terrified of his father that, young as he is, he will gladly remain quiet in any place of concealment when the master of Wuthering Heights is around and in one of his tempers. But the sullen and suspicious Hindley discovers what Mrs. Dean is doing, removes the child from the hiding place, tries clumsily to calm him, and only ends by growing furious and making him cry. Enraged even further by Hareton's tears, Hindley threatens to "crop" the boy, and hauls him screaming up the stairs, pausing only to dangle the child over the banister in order to terrify him even more thoroughly. Suddenly, Hindley loses his grip on his son, and by an ironic stroke of fortune, Heathcliff, passing by at the crucial moment, instinctively reaches out and catches the falling infant. Later Heathcliff will have reason to curse the impulsive gesture that robbed him of a chance to give pain to the detested Hindley. But Hindley is troubled for only a moment by what has happened. Almost immediately he returns to the bottle, still determined to destroy himself, and Heathcliff's only regret, as he and Nelly and the children are ordered drunkenly from Hindley's sight, is that Earnshaw has not yet managed to achieve his suicidal goal.

Nelly puts Hareton to sleep in the kitchen, supposing that Heathcliff has returned to the barn. But actually he has settled himself on a bench near the wall where he cannot be seen, but where he can hear everything that goes on. Cathy enters now to confide in Mrs. Dean that she cannot decide whether or not to marry Edgar Linton. After their quarrel that afternoon, Edgar had proposed and she had accepted him, but now she wants approval for her act, for she feels in her head or in her heart—"in whichever place the soul lives"—that she has done wrong.

She can only explain her love for Linton in the superficial terms of money and position, but her love for Heathcliff is part of her innermost being. I love him, she says, "because he's more myself than I am. Whatever our souls are made of, his and mine are the same." Still, to marry Heathcliff, she believes, would degrade her, and so she has accepted Edgar.

Having heard this, Heathcliff steals out of the kitchen. He leaves Wuthering Heights and does not return. Catherine stays up all night in the rain waiting for her friend to come home, grieved very deeply by his absence, and finally falling ill with a fever. It is not to be expected that she will be a good patient, but she is strong-willed and survives the illness. She spends part of her convalescence with the Lintons at Thrushcross Grange, but the visit is an unlucky one: soon after she arrives at the Grange, Mr. and Mrs. Linton also come down with fever and soon after both are dead. Returning to the Heights, Cathy is spoiled outrageously by her brother, who is anxious for a union with the Lintons, and by the rest of the household, mindful of the doctor's warning that disturbing her might bring back the fever. Nelly, however, steadfastly blames the girl for Heathcliff's disappearance, and Cathy, now more violent and arrogant than ever, treats the housekeeper coldly. Three years later, with Heathcliff still not returned, Catherine and Edgar Linton marry in Gimmerton Chapel, and Nelly follows the girl to Thrushcross Grange, reluctantly leaving the five-year-old Hareton with his father.

Here Mrs. Dean, glancing up at the clock, discovers to her amazement that it is after one. She insists that it is time for Mr. Lockwood to sleep, and both agree to put off the rest of the story until another time.

COMMENT

The central incident in this long chapter is Cathy's description of her love for Heathcliff. The two are united, she says, by an almost mystical bond; in their souls, where they are most themselves, they are most alike. "If all else perished, and he remained," she says, "I should still continue to be; and if all else remained, and he were annihilated, the universe would turn to a mighty stranger." Cathy's decision to betray her profoundest values for the superficial ones of wealth and physical beauty precipitates the tragedy of *Wuthering Heights*. The inner truth that Cathy seeks to ignore for the respectability which her life at the Heights and her visits to the Grange have taught her to crave, is a kind of fierce energy which will twist and torture the inhabitants of both houses until it can be given freer and healthier expression in the love of Hareton and the second Catherine. The destructive passion which Cathy introduces into quiet Thrushcross Grange—symbolically the Lintons die of the fever which the girl brings there and she herself survives—can only be purged by twenty years of suffering.

CHAPTER 10

Four weeks pass, and Lockwood begins to regret in earnest his experiment with solitude. He has been ill all this time, is tired of the gloom and loneliness of the countryside, and is not at all cheered by Dr. Kenneth's statement that he must not expect to be up and about until Spring. One day Heathcliff comes for an hour's visit, bringing with him a gift of some grouse, and his appearance reminds the sick man of the story Nelly Dean had begun a month before. At his first opportunity he calls the housekeeper in, asks her if she will continue the history of Wuthering Heights, and gets her consent.

For a while, Nelly says, after the marriage of Edgar and Cathy, life goes on smoothly at Thrushcross Grange. Both Edgar and Isabella defer to the new wife in everything, and for her part, Cathy seems almost too fond of the brother and sister. She still has occasional fits of passion, but these her husband explains away as aftermaths of her illness. The repose at the Grange is almost unnatural, however, and it comes to an end one September evening when, after a three-year absence, Heathcliff suddenly reappears. The returning Heathcliff is very different from the one who ran away. He has matured, grown tall and more subdued, and there is new intelligence in his eyes.

The feeling of passionate release with which Cathy greets Heathcliff contrasts markedly with Edgar's own coolness and even angers the new husband, suggesting, as it does, how much of his wife's nature has remained unfulfilled in her marriage. Heathcliff, equally delighted and ignoring Edgar's reaction, tells Cathy of how his desire to improve himself had been inspired only by her, of how he would never permit himself to be driven away again, and of how he had been ready to settle his score at once with Hindley and then kill himself to escape the law until his warm reception at the Grange momentarily put such thoughts out of his head. After an hour or two of continued enthusiasm on Cathy's part and continued annoyance on Edgar's, Heathcliff leaves, telling Nelly of his intention to accept Hindley's invitation to stay at Wuthering Heights. As far as Nelly is concerned, Heathcliff would have done better to stay away.

That night Cathy wakens Nelly to share her happiness with her. She confesses that of late she had begun to tire of those spoiled children, Edgar and Isabella, but that with Heathcliff's return, she was now ready to make amends to her husband, her faith restored in both God and man. She does not share Nelly's apprehensions about Heathcliff going to live at the Heights. He has told her, she says, that he plans to offer liberal payment for a room there, so that he can be close to the Grange, and that Hindley is too miserly to turn down such an offer. And after all, what could Heathcliff do to harm Hindley that Hindley has not already done to himself?

The next day, Edgar permits Isabella and Catherine to go to Wuthering Heights, and Heathcliff, returning the visit on several occasions, does not presume on the privilege. He does not want to exhaust Edgar's patience by pressing his attention on his wife, but Edgar has more than Cathy to think about now. Isabella, it seems, has become suddenly and irresistibly attracted to Heathcliff; and her brother, knowing that if he should die without a male heir his property will pass to his sister's husband, does not want Isabella even to think of marrying this nameless man whose character he cannot really bring himself to believe has changed.

Catherine adds her own warnings about Heathcliff's bitter, ambitious nature, but Isabella now insists that she loves him. Catherine even goes so far as to reveal Isabella's feeling to Heathcliff in her sister-in-law's presence, and Heathcliff's first reaction is, not unexpectedly, contempt. But later, he asks Cathy if Edgar's property would not come to him as Isabella's husband, though the new mistress of Thrushcross Grange dismisses the subject with a reminder that Edgar's property is hers. Heathcliff becomes ominously thoughtful during the rest of the events. Nelly Dean is still uneasy about the newly returned young man, wishing he had stayed away. She thinks of Hindley at Wuthering Heights alone with Heathcliff as a stray sheep abandoned by God to an evil beast.

COMMENT

This chapter dramatically portrays Cathy's discontent with her lot at Thrushcross Grange by showing her elation at the return of Heathcliff. Full of comparatively good manners on everybody's part, it is nevertheless also full of foreboding. Heathcliff tells us, for example, that he has been dissuaded from killing both Hindley and himself, but it takes little imagination on the reader's part to guess that something like this is going to happen sooner or later. What's more, Heathcliff's musings about Isabella and her brother's property are hardly reassuring. It is plain that he, like Cathy, has acquired only a superficial appearance of respectability, and that his real nature stands ready at any moment to break through the pretense of civility.

Chapter 10 is also notable for its precise information about the inheritance laws of the day. Many early critics attacked Emily Brontë for being too wild, too grotesquely passionate, and too unaware of "the real world." But Brontë's knowledge of such dry matters as the laws by which property was communicated in nineteenth-century England suggests a very strong grip on the reality that some overly conventional readers claimed was missing in her work.

CHAPTER 11

The chapter continues Nelly Dean's premonitions of disaster for Hindley. Out walking one fall day on her way to Gimmerton, the housekeeper pauses at a signpost where she and Hindley had played together as children, and thinking she sees an apparition of Earnshaw's face, she takes the vision as an omen of death for the master of Wuthering Heights. Frightened, she hurries to the Heights for confirmation of her fears, and there meets Hareton, the little brown-eyed boy who, until ten months before, had been in her care. Hareton seems not to recognize Nelly, and every second word he speaks is a curse. Mr. Heathcliff, it seems, has forbidden the curate to continue instructing the boy, and has undertaken to degrade the child as he himself was degraded and to teach Hareton to hate his father.

When Heathcliff makes his next visit to Thrushcross Grange, he finds Isabella outside and, not realizing that he is being observed by Nelly, tries to kiss the girl. Isabella runs off frightened, and the housekeeper, shocked to see Heathcliff making love to a woman for whom she has often heard him express his contempt, mutters "Judas! Traitor!" loud enough to be overheard by Catherine. When Heathcliff comes into the house, he and Cathy begin to quarrel over Isabella. Cathy says that if Heathcliff were really fond of the girl (which she does not believe he is), she would personally see to it that Edgar permitted the marriage. This statement angers Heathcliff, who accuses Catherine of being jealous and of behaving "infernally" to him. Cathy knows, he says, that if he wanted to marry Isabella he would not wait around for Linton's approval; thus her statement—that she would help to bring the marriage about—has been made only to torture Heathcliff with a pretended indifference to such a match.

Nelly is shocked by the violence of the quarrel and, overestimating its seriousness, she hurries out to inform Edgar, who is angry that he, his wife, and his sister must continue to suffer Heathcliff's indignities. Stationing two servants in a passage to the kitchen, he goes in to dismiss Heathcliff from the house. But Catherine locks the door of the kitchen and forces Edgar to face the intruder's contemptuous bullying on his own. Edgar is obviously terrified, but is goaded to such fury by Heathcliff's taunts that he hits his opponent in the throat and then makes his escape through the rear entrance. Before the master of Thrushcross Grange can return with the servants, Heathcliff has destroyed the lock on the kitchen door and has left the house through the front.

Cathy is now nearly distracted at having Heathcliff turned out of the house. She tells Nelly that if Edgar will not permit her to keep Heathcliff as a friend, she will torment her husband by deliberately setting out to destroy herself. Nelly is shocked by this cold-blooded determination of Cathy's to use her infirmity to her own advantage, and when Edgar arrives to demand that Cathy choose between him and Heathcliff, causing his wife to fall, apparently, into a terrifying, deathly fit, Nelly tries to reassure her master by explaining that the girl is only pretending to be ill. At this, Catherine leaps up in a wild frenzy and rushes to her room, remaining there for several days without food or companionship. Meanwhile, Edgar, persuaded not to take his wife's behavior seriously, spends his time in the library. On one occasion he speaks with Isabella, trying to get his sister to admit that she is shocked at Heathcliff's advances. But Isabella will not produce the required reaction and Edgar warns her that if she continues to encourage her worthless suitor, he, as her brother, will have nothing more to do with her.

COMMENT

This chapter makes us especially aware of the important fact that Nelly Dean is not a perceptive or trustworthy observer where Catherine and Heathcliff are concerned, and thus warns us that we must be ready to supply our own interpretations for much of the material that she gives us. Nelly, the storyteller, is not what critics would call an "omniscient narrator," whose word must be assumed to be correct at all times. She is instead a limited and fallible human being whose values represent the conventional values of her time and place and who cannot appreciate the special nature of Cathy's and Heathcliff's souls. Thus, it is out of the ironic conflict between events themselves and Nelly's interpretations of them that the story emerges. Indeed, much of the trouble in this chapter and the next stems from Nelly's obtuseness. The woman cannot see, for example, that what would be a deadly quarrel for anyone else is just the way that Cathy and Heathcliff have developed of expressing their tortured love. Nor can she understand that though Cathy's frenzy is calculated, the girl is committed to her course of action to the death. In the same way, her harsh judgments of Heathcliff here, and earlier in the story, result from her narrowness of vision and, incidentally, make possible a sympathy for the tortured, brutal boy and man, which the reader might never have felt had Heathcliff himself been the narrator of the story.

Cathy's refusal to eat, incidentally, introduces one of the most important metaphors of the novel. This fasting by the girl, and Heathcliff's fast at the end of the book, make two points: that there is no earthly food that can satisfy the special craving of the two lovers, and that only by abstaining from such worldly food can they hope to reach the place where they may find their own proper nourishment—one another. Toward this end, of course, they almost literally devour each other throughout the novel.

CHAPTER 12

The next few days are quiet, but full of tension. Isabella spends her time wandering about the grounds of Thrushcross Grange, while Edgar sits in his library waiting for Catherine to abandon her foolish behavior and come to him with an apology. Of course, Catherine has no such intention. On the third day she unlocks her door, but only to ask for some water and gruel. She looks ill and behaves strangely; still, Nelly, under the impression that the girl's sickness is entirely premeditated, continues to vex her with talk of how Edgar has spent nearly the whole two days in philosophical resignation in the library. This news only further enrages Cathy, who swears that if only she could be sure that her death would destroy her husband, she would gladly kill herself. She then returns to her bed and begins to experience increasingly feverish fits of madness. Her outbursts are so violent that Mrs. Dean now starts to wonder if she has not perhaps judged the girl's behavior too hastily. The doctor had, after all, warned that Cathy's fever would return if she were thwarted and now, as she stands before the window she has flung open, the harsh northeast wind biting into her barely covered flesh, she falls into a delirium which frightens even the housekeeper.

She tears her pillow apart and sees, in the pigeon feathers which it contains, a reason for her inability to die. The next moment, however, she catches sight of her face in a mirror (which she thinks is a black clothes press), and when the image refuses to vanish after the stroke of twelve, she becomes frightened and is certain that the reflection is an omen of her approaching death. But her most moving hallucinations are about Wuthering Heights and Heathcliff. She imagines she can see a light across the moors in one of the windows of the Heights and that Joseph is sitting up late waiting to let the young Cathy and Heathcliff in. She thinks that she and her friend have stopped by the churchyard to call up ghosts and she says aloud, as if talking to the boy, "I'll not lie there by myself: they may bury me twelve feet deep, and throw the church down over me, but I won't rest till you are with me. I never will."

At this point Edgar comes in and is appalled to see Catherine's condition and to hear her prophesy that by next spring she will be dead, lying under a headstone where Linton (whose ancestors lie in the chapel) may choose to join her or not as he pleases. Edgar is angry with Nelly for her concealment from him of the facts of his wife's condition, and having told her what he thinks of her judgment, he sends the housekeeper out to fetch Mr. Kenneth, the doctor. Outside, Nelly finds Isabella's pet dog hanging from a bridle hook in the wall, and thinks she hears the sound of hoofbeats rushing away in the distance. Later, escorting the doctor to the Grange, she learns that what Heathcliff had been doing in the garden three days before was urging Isabella to run off with him, and that the poor girl, to postpone the act, had promised to be ready the next time she was asked. Back at the house, Nelly looks into Isabella's room and finds it empty, but chooses not to be the bearer of more bad news to Edgar. The next morning, therefore, the brother learns of his sister's elopement from a maid who tells of how the couple had been seen the previous evening some miles past Gimmerton getting a horse's shoes attended to. Edgar's reaction is in character. He receives the information sadly but quietly, saying that he will not try to search for his sister and that her possessions are to be sent on to her new home as soon as she communicates with the Grange.

COMMENT

Cathy's delirium is one of the lyric high-points of the book, one of the scenes which make *Wuthering Heights* unique among English novels. There is here that sense of madness raised to the level of a higher sanity that we get only in such other great moments in literature as the hovel scene in Shakespeare's *King Lear*. Central to Cathy's vision is her mystical feeling of unity with Heathcliff and her desperate sense that because of the way fate has framed their lives, they can, in this world, experience love only through giving and receiving pain. Such an idea is far outside the conventional system of values of the other characters in the book; and as we have seen, the tragedy of *Wuthering Heights* is a function of the conflict between such conventions and the unique, unfathomable, haunted relationship of Heathcliff and Cathy. In plot terms, the delirious vision of this chapter helps to explain Heathcliff's calling into the night for Cathy in Chapter 3, and the bitter man's overwhelming desire, at the end of the story, to rejoin his lost love.

Chapter 12 also advances Heathcliff's grand plan of revenge, for by marrying Isabella he both pains Edgar and paves the way for his later acquisition of Thrushcross Grange. Taken together with the deliberate degradation of Hindley and Hareton, the elopement only helps more fully to establish the demonic depths of the man's bitterness. The hanging of Isabella's pet dog makes the same point in a single gesture. It must be remembered that the first time Heathcliff ever saw Isabella and Edgar, the two were quarreling over a lap dog. Thus, this senseless brutality suggests how carefully Heathcliff has stored up every memory of his enemies, the better to torment them. The hanging of the dog also looks forward to Hareton's similar viciousness in a later chapter and will suggest there how successful Heathcliff has been in fashioning the boy in his own image.

CHAPTER 13

Two months pass, and Isabella and Heathcliff do not return. Edgar, however, has much to occupy him besides his sister. He spends all of his time and energy caring for Catherine, and through his gentleness and devotion, the girl rallies and throws off the worst effects of what has been diagnosed as "brain fever," a nearly universal, if somewhat vaguely defined, nineteenth-century malady, especially common in novels. He labors at his wife's cure even though the doctor has assured him that he is wasting his vitality and undermining his own health in the service of "a mere ruin of humanity."

One day at the beginning of March, Edgar comes in from a walk carrying a bunch of early yellow crocuses which he places on Cathy's pillow. Cathy is pleased with the flowers and, heartened by them, gets out of bed for the first time since her attack. Edgar talks to his wife about the fresh spring air on the hills and longs for the day when she can go there herself to enjoy it. But returning health has not dispelled Cathy's gloom. She announces to her husband that when she goes to the hills, she will go only once and will not return. Nevertheless, she agrees to spend the day in the parlor, where a fire is lit for her. By evening she is exhausted. It is decided that a bedroom should be prepared for her downstairs. Edgar is especially anxious that his wife not waste her strength because she is soon to have a baby, perhaps a boy to stand between Thrushcross Grange and the vengeful Heathcliff.

Six weeks after leaving the Grange with Heathcliff, Isabella writes to her brother about her marriage in a rather formal letter. The letter includes, however, a frightened, apologetic postscript that hints at the sister's desperate need for friendship and help. Edgar doesn't reply to the letter, and two weeks later Isabella writes again, this time to Nelly. In the second letter she reveals the horror and desperation of life at the Heights. Heathcliff, she fears, is mad; Hindley, recognizing that he is being cheated out of his property and will have nothing to leave to his son, Hareton, awaits an opportunity for murder; and Heathcliff, hating Edgar for "causing" Cathy's illness and not having the brother before him to torment, takes his fury out on the sister. Isabella needs more than anything else a friendly face and a sympathetic listener, and she begs Nelly to visit her soon.

COMMENT

The irony here is in the fact that the coming of spring, the expected birth of a baby, and Catherine's recovery are all really preludes to the girl's death. The crocuses which Edgar brings in from the hills are full of life and promise, suggestive of the normal world in which Linton lives and from which Catherine and Heathcliff are forever barred. Needless to say, Cathy cannot accept her husband's tender invitation into this world, assuring him that only death will ever permit her to enter it. And it is a fact that the death-haunted people in this novel are far more powerful than the more conventional characters. Thus, if Cathy's presence at Thrushcross Grange is enough to blight the lives of everyone there, poor Isabella's mere presence at Wuthering Heights is hardly enough to alter the deadly, corrupting atmosphere of that place, an atmosphere which twists and withers both the trees that surround the house and the people who live inside.

CHAPTER 14

Edgar does not object when Nelly asks permission to go to Wuthering Heights to visit Isabella. Nevertheless, he refuses to send along a note of forgiveness for his sister, explaining that there is nothing to forgive. He's not angry with the girl, he says, but feels that nothing should pass between the families. When Nelly arrives at the Heights, she is shocked at the way Isabella has changed. While Heathcliff looks like a born and bred gentleman, his wife seems to have degenerated into a "little slattern." Isabella is on the verge of tears when she learns that Edgar has not written to her. But Heathcliff, ignoring his wife's misery, immediately begins to question Mrs. Dean about Catherine.

Nelly tries to convince Heathcliff not to see Catherine again, but it is hardly possible for her to succeed in this attempt. Heathcliff, managing at first to suppress his eagerness and rage, asks Nelly to arrange a meeting for him with Catherine. The housekeeper suggests that one more meeting like the last one might kill her mistress. She claims that, in any case, Cathy has nearly forgotten her former friend. However, Heathcliff refuses to accept her story. Life would be hell for him, he says, if Catherine's love were dead. As for himself, his love for her in one day, he announces, is greater than eighty years of Edgar's watery affection.

Isabella cannot remain silent at this affront, but the moment she speaks up, her husband cruelly reminds her that even her own brother has abandoned her. Nelly tries to defend Isabella, mentioning that she looks "sadly the worse" for her move from the Grange to the Heights. Heathcliff reacts to this defense by becoming openly vicious. He reminds his wife that he had never tried to conceal his real character from her—that he had told her, for example, when he was hanging her dog on the night of their elopement, that he longed to see everything associated with her and Thrushcross Grange, except Catherine, hanged in the same way. It was Isabella, Heathcliff continues, who had insisted upon seeing in her future husband qualities which didn't exist. If she is suffering now, she is paying the price for her own delusions. The husband has done nothing illegal, Heathcliff insists, and so the wife has no right to complain, though she is free to go whenever she wishes.

Nelly is shocked at what she speaks of as Heathcliff's madness, and asks Isabella why she stays in the same house with him. The girl replies that Heathcliff's offer to let her go is a lie, like everything else "the monster" says. She has already tried to escape and doesn't dare to repeat the experiment. She knows that her husband is trying to reduce her to cringing despair as a way of taking revenge on Edgar, and the only pleasure she can conceive of now is to die or to see Heathcliff dead.

Sardonically, Heathcliff calls Nelly's attention to this outburst of his wife's. He is gratified that in so short a time he has succeeded in breaking her spirit. Clearly, she can no longer be permitted to manage her own affairs, and her husband, as guardian, must exercise full control. He orders her from the room and, once alone with Nelly, tries to convince the housekeeper to help him visit Catherine. The girl who, he says, must feel that she is in hell, trapped in a strange house and driven to distraction by Edgar's weak pity. At first, Nelly resists, but in the end she agrees to take a letter from Heathcliff to Catherine when she returns to the Grange.

At this point in the story, as Mr. Kenneth, the doctor, arrives, Nelly breaks off and leaves Lockwood alone. He speculates about his growing preoccupation with Cathy Heathcliff and to wonder what would happen if he fell in love with her and she turned out to be a "second edition" of her mother.

COMMENT

The picture we get of life at Wuthering Heights in this chapter balances the picture in Chapter 13 of life at Thrushcross Grange. Isabella, transplanted, like Catherine, from her natural environment, is, like her sister-in-law, withering away. Also like Catherine, she can conceive of no pleasure but her own death and that of Heathcliff. Emily Brontë uses the device of breaking off the story at the end of the chapter in part to remind us that we are listening to a narrative told by one of the participants in the drama.

CHAPTER 15

A week later, Nelly Dean takes up the story again, and Lockwood repeats it for the reader substantially in the housekeeper's own words.

Nelly, returning to Thrushcross Grange after her visit to the Heights, hesitates to present Heathcliff's letter to Catherine while Edgar is in the house because she does not know how her mistress will react to it. On the other hand, it disturbs her to withhold the letter because she senses Heathcliff's presence at the Grange and is anxious to avoid further pressure from him. Finally, on a Sunday, four days after the visit to Isabella, Nelly sees her opportunity. The family has gone to church, one remaining servant is sent to the village to buy oranges, and, having left the doors and windows open for the inevitable visitor, the housekeeper brings the letter up to Catherine's room.

Seated quietly by her window, Catherine is dressed in white, her recently cut hair falling simply and naturally on her neck and forehead. She seems to have acquired an other-worldly beauty which marks her out for death, even as more prosaic signs suggest a successful convalescence. Nelly speaks of having a letter but Catherine does not respond. Only when the housekeeper mentions Heathcliff's name does the woman stir and begin to read the brief note. And when she learns that Heathcliff himself is downstairs, longing to see her, her eagerness lights up her face as she strains to catch the sound of his footsteps on the stairs.

Heathcliff hurries into the room, takes Catherine in his arms and, when the woman kisses him, returns the kiss a hundred times. Understanding at a glance that Cathy is doomed, Heathcliff can hardly bring himself to look at her. "Oh, Cathy! Oh, my life! how can I bear it?" he cries. Cathy is angry with him, however, for having—together with Edgar—helped to destroy her and then requiring her pity for their distress. "I care nothing for your sufferings," she exclaims bitterly. "Why shouldn't you suffer? I do." And—half mad with fury—she goes on to torture Heathcliff with a picture of how "happy" he will be with "others" (presumably a new love, as well as a whole family of children!) after she's gone. Heathcliff, himself "savagely" moved by jealous ardor, demands to know if she's "possessed with a devil" to talk so to him when she's dying. "Is it not sufficient for your infernal selfishness that while you are at peace I shall writhe in the torments of hell?" he cries.

A moment later Cathy relents and begs Heathcliff not to nurse his anger at her (for her marriage to Linton), for that will be worse to remember than her own harsh words. But when Heathcliff, withdrawing silently to the other side of the room, shows no sign of complying with her wishes, she muses that, after all, what "irks" her most is "this shattered prison" of her body. Though she must leave Heathcliff, and though, worse, she apparently must leave him on a note of discord, she is not sorry to die; the limitations of the flesh bother her now more than anything.

In a strain of almost mystic ecstasy, she declares that "I'm wearying to escape into that glorious world (of the pure spirit) and to be always there." And when she is there, she concludes, after her death she will be "incomparably beyond and above" all those who, "in full health and strength," like Nelly, pity her now.

At this point the finality of the separation from Cathy which confronts him seems to reawaken all of Heathcliff's passion, and before Nelly can even see him move, the two are in each other's arms, locked in a wild embrace. Indeed, Heathcliff now clasps his beloved with such mad intensity that the prosaic Nelly hardly feels "as if I were in the company of a creature of my own species." Humbled, as only Catherine can humble him, and shattered by the force of his emotion, he begs, "Why did you despise me? Why did you betray your own heart?" Catherine replies, sobbing, that "If I've done wrong, I'm dying for it." The pair remain silent for a moment, weeping quietly. Nelly remarks unsympathetically that "it seemed Heathcliff could weep on a great occasion."

But soon, as the afternoon wears on, the time comes for Edgar to return from church services. The worried housekeeper warns Catherine and Heathcliff of his imminent arrival. A moment later, Linton himself opens the gate and starts up the walk to the house. Nelly begs Heathcliff to hurry away, but when he tries to leave Cathy clasps him even tighter and refuses to let him go. Alarmed, he tries to break away, but when the woman hysterically exclaims that she'll die if he leaves her, Heathcliff prepares to remain and confront her husband, with Catherine still in his arms. Desperately, Nelly (who doesn't want to appear to have been treacherous to Edgar) tries to persuade him to get up and go or he'll "ruin" all three, "master, mistress, and servant," But her efforts meet with no success. She notes with relief, though, that Catherine seems to be unconscious. "She's fainted or dead," she thinks, and better so than "a misery-maker" as she is now. At this moment, Edgar enters, and turns white with astonishment and rage at the sight of Heathcliff and Catherine. Heathcliff, however, prevents whatever action the other might have meant to take by placing the "lifeless-looking" woman in his arms, exclaiming, "unless you be a fiend, help her first." He then retires to the parlor.

Edgar, anxious about his wife, momentarily forgets Heathcliff's presence. But Nelly, who remembers it only too well, takes the first opportunity to seek him out and beg him to leave the house. Heathcliff agrees to go outside, but insists on spending the night in the garden so that he can be near by. After extracting a promise from Nelly that she will let him know how her mistress is first thing in the morning, he delivers the house, as the servant puts it, "of his luckless presence."

COMMENT

This is one of the climatic chapters of the book; here is the secret center of the novel toward which we have been moving ever since Lockwood's first, hesitant introduction of himself to the inhabitants of Wuthering Heights. As Catherine and Heathcliff meet for the last time, the reality of their terrible love extinguishes every other emotion in the book, even Heathcliff's subsequent passion for revenge. Their love, every expression of which seems torn from their living flesh, is as primal and savage as the moors themselves. Again and again the lovers insists upon their inseparability, and with terrible yet pitiable perverseness swear to torment one another until they can be together forever in death. Heathcliff accuses Catherine of having forsaken her innermost nature in abandoning him, and here we find what has been called one of the central themes of *Wuthering Heights.* Nowhere else in the novel is Emily Brontë so completely the lyric and dramatic poet. One would have to turn to Richard Wagner's opera, *Tristan and Isolde*, where, too, the lovers pray for night and death to unite them forever, to find so musical a treatment of human passion and despair.

CHAPTER 16

At twelve o'clock on the night following the reunion of Heathcliff and Catherine, the young Catherine—whose acquaintance Lockwood has made at Wuthering Heights—is born. Two hours later her mother dies without ever regaining consciousness.

Edgar Linton is, of course, in despair at his wife's death; and Nelly, herself grieving for Catherine, considers the situation doubly painful because since he has been left without a male heir, his entire estate—upon the event of his death—will now be left to Isabella and—through her—to Heathcliff.

Nelly relates that Edgar's new daughter—who is at least in part the cause of all this trouble—was pretty much neglected in the period immediately following her mother's death. Edgar, in "exhausted anguish," has taken up a station beside his dead wife, who seems—as she herself had predicted—overwhelmingly peaceful and beautiful compared to those left behind. At the earliest opportunity—"soon after sunrise"—Nelly steals outside, ostensibly for a breath of air. In reality, she intends to inform Heathcliff of the events of the night.

She finds him stationed motionless among the larches in the garden, and from his despairing stance it is plain that he has already heard the news. "She's dead," he tells Nelly, "I've not waited for you to learn that." The servant, ordinarily so hostile to Heathcliff, can't help pitying him. "A foolish notion struck me that his heart was quelled, and he prayed, because his lips moved, and his gaze was bent on the ground," she tells us. But when she tries to comfort him with empty reassurances about heaven, he replies with a half-sneer and asks only to know how Catherine had died. Again, Nelly tries to comfort Heathcliff by telling him that it was "quietly as a lamb," but this seems to enrage rather than reassure the distracted lover. He responds with a desperate outcry which ominously foreshadows the shape of things to come—the course of the rest of his life as well as the nature of his death. "May she wake in torment!" he exclaims. "I pray one prayer—I repeat it till my tongue stiffens—Catherine Earnshaw, may you not rest as long as I am living! You said I killed you—haunt me then! . . . Be with me always—take any form—drive me mad! only do not leave me in this abyss, where I cannot find you! Oh God! it is unutterable! I cannot live without my life! I cannot live without my soul!" And with these words, to Nelly's horror, the passionate man dashes his head against the trunk of a tree and howls, "not like a man, but like a savage beast getting goaded to death with knives and spears." Furthermore, it is obvious from the bloodstains on the tree trunk and on Heathcliff that he has been doing this all night. Appalled and helpless, Nelly departs.

Catherine's funeral has been arranged for the Friday following her death. In the meantime, her coffin remains in the great drawing-room and Linton watches continually beside it, "a sleepless guardian." Heathcliff, equally sleepless, watches without, in the garden. Only on Tuesday, when Edgar has retired for a few hours from sheer exhaustion, is Nelly able to let Heathcliff in briefly for a last farewell to his love. Afterward, the servant discovers that he has replaced the light strand of Edgar's hair in Catherine's locket with a dark one of his own. Nelly recovers Linton's curl and, twisting the two together, encloses both, as a symbol, perhaps, of the division between these two elements in the dead girl herself.

As for the funeral, Nelly relates that Hindley Earnshaw was, of course, invited, but failed to attend. Only Edgar and his tenants and servants accompany Catherine to the grave. To everyone's surprise, the girl is buried, not in the Linton chapel nor in the Earnshaw family plot, but in a new spot, dug on a green slope in a quiet corner of the churchyard where the moor flowers grow over the wall.

COMMENT

Catherine's death at once ends the first half of the novel and begins the second. The chapter is full of foreshadowing.

1) The birth of Catherine Linton introduces a new member of the second generation at the Heights and the Grange, the generation that will restore the order the first generation so violently disturbed.

2) Nelly's gloom at the thought that Edgar's estate might pass to Heathcliff, because Edgar's wife had died without giving him a son, prepares the reader for this later development.

3) Heathcliff's furious cry to Catherine to be with him always both explains the events of Lockwood's dream in Chapter 4 and sets the scene for the final incidents of the book.

4) Finally, Catherine's burial on a green slope in a corner of the churchyard, instead of beside her relatives or those of her husband, is suggestive of a return to the moors to which she was so attached, and of which she was so much a creature. The burial also readies the reader for the glimpse, on the last page of the book, of the three graves side by side.

CHAPTER 17

Immediately after Catherine's funeral, the spring rains begin to fall. Edgar keeps to his room, and the next afternoon, when Nelly sits in the lonely parlor rocking his premature daughter, she hears laughter behind her. Turning with a sharp reprimand on her lips, she discovers to her astonishment that the intruder is "Mrs. Heathcliff," the former Isabella Linton. Most of the rest of this chapter is taken up with Isabella's story of her escape from Wuthering Heights. But first Nelly gets the exhausted woman—who is not only rain-drenched but bleeding from a cut on her neck—into fresh clothes, and orders the carriage brought round to take her on to Gimmerton. Isabella insists on leaving almost immediately, lest Heathcliff follow her to the Grange and make further trouble for her and her brother.

The story she tells is a wild one, made even more so by the extent of her own bitterness and hatred of her husband. She declares that "he has extinguished my love effectually." Indeed, when Nelly remonstrates that there are worse men than Heathcliff who, after all, is genuinely suffering because of his grief for his adored Catherine, Isabella angrily retorts that "He's not a human being . . . and he has no claim on my charity—I gave him my heart, and he took and pinched it to death . . . and since he has destroyed [it], I have not power to feel for him, and I would not, though he groaned from this to his dying day, and wept tears of blood for Catherine."

Isabella continues that Hindley, too, is consumed by a powerful desire for revenge against Heathcliff. Though he tried to keep sober for his sister's funeral, he couldn't. By nightfall on Friday he was drunk to a point just "below irrationality." In the gloomy twilight, he and Isabella waited alone by the fire for Heathcliff's return from the churchyard. But when Heathcliff appeared unexpectedly early and couldn't open the kitchen door (which had already been latched by Joseph), it occurred to Hindley to lock him out of the main entrance, too. Isabella went along with this idea. But when Hindley suggested that they ought to avenge themselves once and for all by murdering Heathcliff, she became alarmed and ran to the window to warn him that Hindley was planning to shoot him. Heathcliff replied snarling that she'd better open the door, but Isabella refused to "meddle" in the men's quarrel any further, smugly remarking that she'd done her duty. At this point, she was cursed by both Hindley (for having betrayed his purpose) and Heathcliff (for not letting him in). But a moment later Heathcliff himself managed to smash a window, and appearing threateningly in the frame, demanded that she do his bidding. She refused, tauntingly declaring that it's "a poor love of yours that cannot bear a shower of snow" and daring him to go and die on Catherine's grave "like a faithful dog."

Hindley rushed to the window and in the struggle that

ensued, Heathcliff managed to tear his weapon from him and stab him in the wrist. Then, smashing another window, he leapt into the room and continued kicking and beating the prostrate Hindley till he was almost dead, after which he roughly bound up the unconscious man's wounds and forced the horrified Joseph and the terrified Isabella to do likewise.

The next morning, Isabella continues, she came down at breakfast time to discover Hindley, sick from the aftereffects of his binge and his beating, and Heathcliff, sick with grief, sitting "gaunt and ghastly," without appetite, at the table. "I experienced a certain sense of satisfaction and superiority," she tells Nelly, "as, at intervals, I cast a look towards my silent companions, and felt the comfort of a quiet conscience within me." Heathcliff's features especially, she remarks, were "sealed in an expression of unspeakable sadness." Had he been another she would have pitied him but, she continues (showing the extent to which vengefulness has corrupted her own humanity), in his case she was "gratified." She seized the first opportunity to inform Hindley of Heathcliff's violent attack on him when he lay unconscious the previous evening. Then she tortured Heathcliff with reminiscences of Catherine and of Catherine's fancied contempt for him, until in rage and despair he threw a dinner knife at her. It struck her beneath the ear, causing the wound that Nelly sees now, and she rushed off frightened into the kitchen as Heathcliff, pursuing her, and Hindley, preventing his pursuit, fell "locked together on the hearth."

In her flight through the kitchen, she goes on, she knocked over Hareton, who was hanging a litter of puppies from a chair-back in the doorway. She then raced out onto the moor and across the marshes, always "precipitating" herself "towards the beacon light of the Grange." She concludes bitterly that she would rather "be condemned to a perpetual dwelling in the infernal regions" than spend another night at Wuthering Heights.

After telling Nelly this story, Isabella departs for a new home near London, taking up residence permanently in the south. She never returns to Thrushcross Grange again, though she and her brother do begin a regular correspondence once things are more settled. A few months after her escape, she bears a son—Linton, "an ailing peevish creature." When Heathcliff learns through some servants of her hiding place and the existence of this son, he doesn't "molest" her, but he does swear to Nelly that "I'll have it, when I want it." ("Fortunately," Nelly interjects, "its mother died before the time arrived, some thirteen years after the decease of Catherine.")

Edgar Linton is also transformed by his wife's death. He gives up his office as magistrate, stops going to church, and in general becomes a kind of hermit. Within a short time, however, he finds a new reason for existence in his love for his daughter, called Cathy, to distinguish her from her mother, Catherine. As for Hindley, within six months of his sister's demise he, too, is dead—from alcoholism, apparently. Nelly hears of the event from Edgar Linton and, grieved for her old playmate, rushes up to Wuthering Heights to help with funeral arrangements. It depresses her especially to think that since Hindley died in Heathcliff's debt, his heir, Hareton, is completely in the power of his old enemy who, still driven by his desire for vengeance, gloats that he will now "see if one tree won't grow as crooked as another with the same wind to twist it." And when Edgar Linton demands that Hareton, as his wife's nephew, be placed in his custody, Heathcliff threatens to replace him with his own and Isabella's son Linton, a threat forceful enough to make Edgar abandon the boy to Heathcliff for good. Indeed, as things now stand, Nelly relates, "the guest is now the master of Wuthering Heights" and Hareton, "who should now be the first gentleman in the neighborhood . . . lives in his own house as a servant . . . quite unable to right himself, because of his friendlessness and his ignorance that he has been wronged."

COMMENT

One of the most remarkable incidents in this long, diffuse chapter occurs at the moment when Isabella, fleeing from the room in which her husband had just thrown a knife at her, passes the young Hareton who is hanging a litter of puppies from the back of a chair. The act has many overtones and calls to mind Heathcliff's hanging of Isabella's lap dog on the night of the couple's elopement. The gesture there may have seemed a particularly pointless piece of cruelty, but we must remember that when the young Catherine and Heathcliff first set eyes on Edgar and Isabella Linton, through a window of Thrushcross Grange, the two spoiled children were arguing over a lap dog. We can easily imagine Heathcliff, whose specialty is harboring grudges, hanging Isabella's lap dog in order to mark, symbolically, his destruction of the way of life at the Grange. And what could better show how thoroughly Hareton had been shaped in Heathcliff's image than his act of hanging the litter of puppies from the back of the chair? Emily Brontë often makes her meaning clear in such indirect ways as this. Toward the end of the chapter, for instance, Heathcliff says to Hareton, "Now, my bonny lad, you are mine! And we'll see if one tree won't grow as crooked as another, with the same wind to twist it." The metaphor, in which Heathcliff refers to himself as a twisted tree, is clearly a reference to the stunted vegetation around Wuthering Heights. This fact suggests that, for Heathcliff, it is not so much his outsmarting of Hindley as his long apprenticeship to the warping passions of the Heights that has made him its true owner.

CHAPTER 18

"The twelve years after Catherine's death were the happiest of my life," Nelly remarks. In this period, she is completely absorbed in bringing up young Cathy, who she describes as "the most winning thing that ever brought sunshine into a desolate house." High-spirited but basically sensitive and gentle, the little girl has her mother's intense dark eyes and her father's fair skin, small features, and curly blonde hair. Spoiled and sheltered by her indulgent father and the adoring Nelly, she has a tendency to be headstrong, counter-balanced by a profound desire to please her father.

Until she reaches the age of thirteen, Cathy is not allowed to leave the Park. She never hears of Wuthering Heights or Heathcliff, and even the nearby town of Gimmerton is "an unsubstantial name in her ears." As she gets older, however, she begins to wonder about her surroundings, and eventually questions Nelly about Penniston Crags, a heap of rocks on the moor near Wuthering Heights, which she sees daily from her window, gleaming in the sunset. Nelly tries to discourage her curiosity, but another maid only excites it further by telling her about the "Fairy Cave," also in that area. Soon, "Now am I old enough to go to Penniston Crags?" is a constant question on Cathy's lips, but she is strictly forbidden to take the trip by her father and her nurse.

In the meantime, Isabella is taken sick in her new home near London. She is convinced that the course of her illness (a feverish consumption) must be fatal, and so she sends for her brother, hoping to entrust the delicate thirteen-year-old Linton to his care and keep him out of Heathcliff's hands. Edgar leaves Cathy with Nelly and departs for three weeks. While he is gone, the faithful servant tries her best to watch over the girl but, trusting her implicitly, allows her to do quite a lot of solitary rambling.

One day Cathy goes off on a little jaunt by herself, asserting that she's "an Arabian merchant, going to cross the Desert with his caravan." Taking her pony, three dogs, and a picnic lunch, she sets out across the moor, promising to be back for tea. But when teatime arrives Cathy has not returned The alarmed Nelly rushes off to look for her. She fears the worst—

that the child has headed for Penniston Crags and through some mishap stumbled instead into the farmhouse at Wuthering Heights—and her fears soon prove true. Arriving at Wuthering Heights, she finds Cathy seated within, merrily chatting with Hareton, now a husky boy of eighteen who, since Heathcliff deliberately failed to educate him, understands little of what the girl is saying. Nelly is relieved to find her charge safe, but apprehensive about what would happen if Heathcliff should discover her there, or Edgar should learn about the adventure. Feigning anger at Cathy's disobedience, she orders her to prepare to leave at once. The child saucily refuses, and when Nelly finally persuades her to leave, she orders Hareton to bring her pony and dogs, since he has denied being the son of the house. When Hareton, annoyed at being taken for a servant, angrily refuses, Cathy, bewildered, flies into a rage at being disobeyed, and the servant at the Heights, a local woman, reprimands her for treating her "cousin" so badly. Cathy is even more startled and confused at this. She wonders how such an uncouth oaf can be her cousin. Nelly can see that beneath Hareton's rough exterior there is a young man of much natural promise, but Cathy, of course, sees only a poorly dressed, uneducated farmhand. But "papa is gone to fetch my cousin [Linton] from London," she protests. "My cousin is a gentleman's son!"

Nelly is "much vexed" at Cathy and the servant for their mutual revelations. Now the news of Isabella's death and Linton's arrival, which Edgar had hoped to keep from his old enemy, will surely be communicated to Heathcliff. Further, Cathy will no doubt tell her father the tale of her own visit to Wuthering Heights, getting Nelly into even more trouble.

On the way home, Cathy explains how she had happened to stop at Wuthering Heights. Hareton's dog had bitten her dog on the road, and the two cousins met and became friendly in the course of the ensuing scrap. Nelly, still worried about Heathcliff's reaction, makes her promise never to relate the story of this adventure to her father. Fear that the whole episode might end in Nelly's dismissal effectively seals the child's lips for, after all, as Nelly says, she is "a sweet little girl."

COMMENT

The novel divides in two here, with the quick passage of twelve years. Some readers have felt this division to be a flaw in the novel; they claim that with the death of Catherine interest in the book must inevitably slacken. Indeed, the famous Samuel Goldwyn motion picture version of the novel (with Laurence Olivier as Heathcliff) fails to go beyond Chapter 17. The movie version only serves to perpetuate this misreading of the novel. Emily Brontë has painted with great skill and dedication the impact of chaotic human forces on an orderly world. Everything that happens in the first half of the story fairly cries out for a restoration of the lost order, and it is toward such a restoration that the second half of the book inexorably moves. It would make about as much sense to end a mystery story before the solution has been given as to end *Wuthering Heights* before a full and final reconciliation of the warring elements in the narrative.

CHAPTER 19

Soon a letter edged with black proclaims Isabella's death and announces Edgar's return from London with his youthful nephew. Cathy is wild with joy at the idea of welcoming her father and her "real cousin" back to the Grange. As she and Nelly wait at the park gate for the carriage, she dances around impatiently, amusing herself and her nurse with fantasies of what a wonderful companion Linton will be.

When the travelers arrive, Linton is asleep in a corner of the coach, wrapped in a fur-lined cloak as though it were winter. He is a pale, effeminate boy, much like Edgar Linton in looks but with a "sickly peevishness in his aspect" that his uncle never had. Edgar Linton warns his daughter not to overtire her delicate cousin with too many games and other diversions on this first evening, for the boy is tired and not strong. When the boy is wakened, he confirms his uncle's report of his character by crying peevishly and begging to be put to bed. Cathy, charmed by his looks despite his behavior, seems to have resolved to make a pet of him. She babies him, stroking his curls and offering him tea from her saucer. Pleased by her coddling, he eventually manages a faint smile. Indeed, Edgar remarks to Nelly that the sickly boy will do very well if they are able to keep him. "The company of a child his own age will instill new spirit into him soon," he declares.

But the fears of Nelly and Edgar are realized when Joseph arrives from Wuthering Heights with a message from Heathcliff, who demands to have his son brought to him immediately. Bitterly disappointed as he is, Edgar can only promise to send him the boy first thing in the morning. The child's mother had wanted her son to remain under his uncle's guardianship, but, of course, Edgar must concede that a father's claim has priority. At this, Joseph unwillingly departs, but with a muttered threat that if Edgar doesn't keep his promise, Heathcliff himself will come for Linton—"un thrust him aht, if yah darr!" growls the surly old servant.

COMMENT

With the appearance of young Linton, we have made the acquaintance of all three of the second-generation characters in the novel. The similarities between these people and their counterparts in the first generation are striking. Cathy has many of the qualities of her mother, Hareton is as rough and surly as the man who brought him up, and Linton has some of the genteel, refined characteristics we have come to associate with the inhabitants of the Grange. Yet there are differences perhaps even more significant than the similarities.

Hareton seems somehow a less tortured boy than the young Heathcliff, perhaps due to a saving affection for his tormentor. And while Linton obviously belongs to the family whose name he bears, he seems to have exaggerated the nervousness and weakness of Isabella without benefiting from Edgar's cool strength of character. Thus the stage is set for a replaying of the old disaster; only this time the players are somewhat different, and so a possibility exists that the story will not end so tragically.

CHAPTER 20

Mr. Linton orders Nelly to take his nephew up to Wuthering Heights early the next morning, without revealing his whereabouts to Cathy "lest she should be restless and anxious to visit the Heights." The delicate boy is reluctant to be gotten up at five in the morning, and even more upset at the idea of leaving his new home so quickly. Spoiled and peevish as he is, even Nelly cannot help sympathizing with his bewilderment at being suddenly transferred from the care of a kindly uncle to that of a father of whom he has never heard. She tries to soften the blow with delusive promises that his absence will be short, and finally, with the assistance of Edgar, she manages to get the unwilling child out of bed and on his way. Riding along on Minny, Cathy's gentle little pony, Linton begins to show a bit more interest in his destination. "Is Wuthering Heights as pleasant a place as Thrushcross Grange?" he asks. Nelly, hard-put to find an answer to the innocent question, declares that it has a splendid view of the surrounding countryside, and that, though he may find the building old and dark at first, he is sure to have "nice rambles" on the moors with Miss Cathy's other cousin, Hareton Earnshaw. The boy also asks about his father. Nelly's carefully understated reply is that he may not seem so gentle and kind as his uncle at first, but that "naturally he'll be fonder of you than any uncle, for you are his own." When the child wonders why his father never came to see him in London, Nelly tells him that it was never convenient, and that he "shouldn't trouble" Heathcliff with questions on the subject.

When the pair arrive at the Heights, Heathcliff quickly strides outside to inspect his son. Having "stared him into an ague of confusion," Nelly tells us, he uttered a scornful laugh. "God! What a beauty! What a lovely, charming thing!" he exclaims. "Haven't they reared it on snails and sour milk, Nelly? Oh, damn my soul! but that's worse than I expected." Trembling and bewildered, Linton is brought into the house, where he weeps when Heathcliff orders him to approach. But his father plainly doesn't plan to hurt him, assuring Nelly, rather, that he means to be especially kind to the boy since he is the prospective owner of Thrushcross Grange as well as Wuthering Heights, and "I should not wish him to die till I was certain of being his successor"—that is, until Edgar Linton is dead. "Besides, he's mine," asserts Heathcliff, "and I want the triumph of seeing my descendants fairly lord" of the Linton and Earnshaw estates. He has furnished a room for his son in handsome style, he continues, and even hired a tutor to visit the boy three times a week. He only regrets that the ailing, delicate child, so unlike himself, is not "a worthy object of pride," but rather "a whey-faced whining wretch."

A moment later Joseph returns with a bowl of milk-porridge for the new arrival which, however, Linton refuses to eat. Hareton was always satisfied with such victuals, Joseph declares—obviously as scornful of the boy as Heathcliff is—but Heathcliff orders him to bring whatever the lad might fancy. Nelly suggests boiled milk or tea, and when her suggestion is relayed to the housekeeper, she reflects hopefully that perhaps Heathcliff's selfish motives for wanting Linton alive will keep the soft boy safe in this rough household. But as she slips quietly out the door—at a moment when she hopes the child is distracted—she hears him frantically crying, "Don't leave me! I'll not stay here! I'll not stay here!"

COMMENT

The removal of Linton from the Grange to the Heights is a poignant moment of dramatic irony, the sort of irony in which the audience is aware of a truth before the characters in the story are. The weather is lovely, and to the boy all seems auspicious. But when he asks, innocently, if the Heights will be as pleasant as Thrushcross Grange, the reader cannot help but wince at the fate that is so soon to overtake him. Inevitably, the chapter that opened in sunshine and heather-scented air ends with Linton's screams. And between these two events, Heathcliff has made abundantly clear his contempt for the "whey-faced whining wretch" who is his son, and his intention of using the boy as the principal agent of his revenge.

CHAPTER 21

The same day, shortly after Linton has left for his new home, Cathy rises in high glee, eager to renew her friendship with her cousin. When she is told that he had to leave—and not, incidentally, that he is now at nearby Wuthering Heights—she is passionately disappointed. Her father is only able to soothe her with promises that the boy will soon return—"if I can get him."

As time passes, however, the girl gradually forgets her brief acquaintance with Linton and, Nelly points out, when they meet again Cathy hardly recognizes her cousin. Nelly herself, however, does keep tabs on the progress of the boy. Whenever she meets the housekeeper from the Heights in town, she asks about him, and learns that he continues in weak health and is "a tiresome inmate." Heathcliff dislikes the boy, the woman reports, but tries to conceal his antipathy. Still, he can't stand being with him for very long, and so Linton is much alone, spending evenings by himself in the parlor, doing lessons, and often lying in bed all day, prey to numerous coughs, colds, aches and pains. Even she herself, Joseph, and the basically good-natured Hareton are heartily sick of the young invalid's constant demands and complaints.

Several more years elapse without any contact between the cousins, until Cathy reaches the age of sixteen. On her birthday—also, of course, the anniversary of her mother's death—her father usually spends the day alone, in the study, with an evening visit to the churchyard where Catherine is buried. Cathy is therefore left to her own resources, and on this particular day she decides to go with Nelly for a ramble on the edge of the moors. Her father gives permission, provided the pair will be back within the hour. As the two stroll along, Cathy, anxious—so she says—to show her nurse a colony of moor-game, gradually hurries ahead, until, disappearing into a hollow, she has passed from Nelly's view. When she next comes into sight, Nelly can see that she's been detained by two persons, one of them apparently Heathcliff, who is now sharply reproving her for "poaching."

Nelly hurries to join the little group, where she quickly recognizes the other figure as Hareton, who is also soon remembered by Cathy as the young man she met on the day of her Penniston Crags adventure some years earlier. When she mistakes him for Heathcliff's son, Heathcliff invites her back to his house to "meet" his real son. Nelly, desperately anxious to keep the girl from Wuthering Heights—and especially to keep her from finding her long-lost cousin there, forbids her to go. Yet Cathy insists, and before Nelly can stop her she scampers off toward the Heights.

As Nelly and Heathcliff follow, Nelly rebukes Heathcliff for his invitation, pointing out that he knows the visit—and the reunion with Linton—can only lead to trouble. "My design is as honest as possible," Heathcliff replies; "That the two cousins may fall in love and get married. I'm acting generously to your master; his young chit has no expectations, and should she second my wishes, she'll be provided for at once, as joint successor with Linton." To this Nelly objects that if Linton dies Cathy would be his heir, but Heathcliff, who has obviously informed himself very carefully on the subject, answers that he himself is Linton's heir, but "to prevent disputes"—that is, about Edgar's property—"I desire their union and am resolved to bring it about."

Arriving at the house, the pair find Cathy waiting for them at the gate, and Linton, just returned from a walk, standing on the hearth within. The boy has grown tall for his age, but he is still slight and delicately pretty. Though his looks and movements are "very languid," Nelly notes that "there was a grace in his manner that mitigated these defects."

When Cathy realizes that Linton is her cousin—the very Linton whose mysterious departure had so disturbed her three years earlier—she embraces him fondly and then turns affectionately to Heathcliff, who she now infers must be her uncle. The dour Heathcliff, however, suggests that she save her kisses for her cousin. Cathy ignores this rudeness and rushes to hug Nelly, scolding her for not wanting her to come in, and asserting that she and her father will take this walk often in the future. Heathcliff—alarmed—explains that Edgar has "a prejudice" against him, and that she had better not mention these visits to her father. After some discussion of arrangements for future meetings, during which Linton shows himself unwilling to travel to the Grange to see his cousin, Heathcliff suggests that the boy take his cousin for a stroll around the house. But Linton again reveals his weakness and feebleness of disposition, shrinking closer to the fire and away from the visitors. Finally, Hareton is summoned to be Cathy's guide. The girl seems to like him, though later she joins with Linton in poking fun at the "colossal dunce" for his uneducated speech and uncouth ways.

Observing all this byplay among the young people, Heathcliff remarks to Nelly that as far as he's concerned, Hareton, with all his ignorance, is worth a dozen Lintons. In a sense, he's proud of the job he's done in brutalizing the lad because it's such an appropriate revenge against Hindley, who did the same to him. On the other hand, though, he can't help admitting Hareton's good qualities. "Mine," he says of Linton, "has nothing valuable about it; yet I shall have the merit of making it go as far as such poor stuff can go. His had first rate qualities and they are lost." Yet despite all this, he concludes, the boy is "damnably fond of him!"

In the meantime, Linton and Cathy are still engaged in teasing Hareton for his many deficiencies of mind and manner, with the younger boy finding, as Nelly says, "animation enough while discussing Hareton's faults." In this way, Nelly and Cathy pass the whole afternoon, and when the time comes to leave, Nelly—who fears Edgar's displeasure—can find no comfort in Cathy's good spirits.

On the next day the whole story comes out, and Edgar, disturbed and upset at this re-intrusion of Heathcliff into his peaceful routine, tries to explain to Cathy why she must avoid Wuthering Heights. "Mr. Heathcliff dislikes me and is a most diabolical man, delighting to wrong and ruin those he hates," he tells Cathy—but she finds this hard to believe. "Mr. Heathcliff was quite cordial, papa," she protests. Edgar then goes on to tell her how badly Heathcliff treated Isabella, his sister and Linton's mother, in the hope that a concrete example of her uncle-in-law's evil disposition will convince her. Finally she seems to understand, but that evening Nelly finds her in tears because she can't help thinking how disappointed Linton will be when she doesn't appear the next day as she'd promised. Nelly declares that Linton won't care in the least, but Cathy begs to be allowed to write a note to explain her absence. Nelly refuses and forbids the girl to continue the friendship.

Despite Nelly's best efforts, however, Cathy does write the letter, and she manages to send it to Wuthering Heights with a milk-fetcher from the village. For some weeks the correspondence thus established continues undisturbed; Nelly is completely fooled. But gradually the nurse becomes suspicious, and finally she discovers the drawer in which Cathy has been keeping a whole sheaf of adolescent love-letters from her cousin. Investigating further, she learns of the routine whereby Cathy has employed the innocent milk-fetcher as messenger and, after a scene in which she confronts her charge with her new knowledge, the relationship is cut short by a note from Nelly to the Heights stating that "Master Heathcliff is requested to send no more notes to Miss Linton, as she will not receive them." And from then on, the former letter-carrier "came with vacant pockets."

COMMENT

Most significant in this chapter is Heathcliff's summary of his feelings for Linton and Hareton. He holds Linton—the pampered instrument of his revenge—in contempt, even though he is his own son. He sees in the boy the same weakness and passivity that for him has always characterized the inhabitants of Thrushcross Grange. Hareton, on the other hand—the boy he has deliberately brutalized out of hatred for his father—is a source of affection for Heathcliff. This affection, we later learn, is touchingly returned.

CHAPTER 22

As summer draws to an end and autumn settles in the fields, Cathy and her father often walk out among the reapers. On the evening when the last sheaves are gathered, they stay out too long, and Edgar catches a bad cold from the chill, which obliges him to remain indoors for the rest of the winter. Cathy, sad and dull since her romance with Linton was cut short, has been ordered by her father to read less and exercise more, and Nelly feels obliged to keep her company on walks through the park.

One rainy November afternoon as the two are taking their customary stroll, Cathy, in especially low spirits, confides to Nelly her worries about her father's health. He has been worse than usual on this day, and Cathy cannot help brooding on the possibility of his death. The thought of him leaving her, she tells Nelly, is more than she can endure. And even the thought of Nelly's death depresses her, for then she'll be left alone. In a way, however, she hopes that her father will die before she does. Cathy loves him too much to bear the idea of him being as grief-stricken and miserable as she knows he would be if he were the survivor. Nelly tries to cheer the girl up, and then takes advantages of her loving mood to advise her not to give her father any other cause for grief—such as she might by resuming her forbidden correspondence with Linton. Cathy is moved and promises to do Nelly's bidding.

As they talk, the pair approach the wall of the park where a nearby gate opens onto the road outside. Restored to her good spirits by the conversation, Cathy catches sight of a wild rose tree blooming above the wall. She climbs up after some flowers and in so doing loses her hat. But the outside door is locked and she must scramble down the wall to recover it. Once down, however, Cathy finds she is unable to get back, and Nelly begins searching her pockets for a key to the locked entrance.

As Nelly, finding no key, is about to run back home to get one, a rider approaches; it is none other than Heathcliff. Cathy, frightened, refuses to speak to him but he insists on her listening. Since she dropped her correspondence with Linton, he tells her, his son has fallen into a "Slough of Despond." The boy was sincere in his declarations. "As true as I live," Heathcliff maintains, "he's dying for you now—breaking his heart at your fickleness." The cynical Nelly expresses doubt at this sad story, but Heathcliff swears that he is telling the truth and begs Cathy to go to the Heights and see for herself. He will be away for all of the coming week, he says, and surely

Edgar himself could have no objection to his daughter visiting her sick cousin.

While Heathcliff is talking, Nelly manages to open the gate, and as soon as he finishes his speech and rides off, she hurries her charge inside as a hard rain begins and there is no more time for talk. Once home, however, Cathy is plunged again into despair—now doubly dark because her worries over Linton are added to her anxiety for her father. She can never feel at ease, she tells Nelly, till she knows whether or not Heathcliff's assertions are true. Finally, the reluctant Nelly—unable to stand the girl's silent sorrow—agrees to accompany her to Wuthering Heights. They set off for the Heights the next morning as Nelly yields to her charge's wishes "in the faint hope that Linton himself might prove, by his reception of us, how little of the tale was founded in fact."

COMMENT

This chapter contains an ironic commentary on the nature of evil. In order to bend Catherine to his will, Heathcliff makes use of the girl's natural human sympathy for Linton and her love for her father. This, the incident seems to suggest, is the tribute that evil must always pay to goodness. For in the very act of doing wrong, a wicked man must acknowledge the existence of the right and even its superiority. It is, of course, just this affectionate nature of Cathy's which, in the end, will frustrate Heathcliff's darkest design and restore life to Wuthering Heights.

CHAPTER 23

The day is cold and damp, but Cathy and Nelly nevertheless brave the chill to journey to the Heights. Nelly is cross and bad-tempered because her feet are thoroughly wet. The two enter the farmhouse through the kitchen to be sure Heathcliff is really absent. They find the dour Joseph enjoying himself by the fire with a quart of ale and some roasted oat-cakes.

Heathcliff is indeed away, but in the next room they can hear Linton peevishly calling for the old servant to come and poke up his fire. Joseph ignores the boy, so Cathy and Nelly hurry to his aid.

Cathy, of course, greets her cousin with the utmost fondness—but she is rebuffed by the invalid, who complains that her kisses take his breath away. "Why didn't you come before?" he inquires fretfully. He then issues querulous orders to his visitors—fix the fire, bring some water, call Zillah (the housekeeper), etc. Nelly only restrains herself from rebuking him for his bad manners by reminding herself how sick he is.

Cathy tries to comfort Linton and affectionately declares that she wishes he were her brother. But Linton—thoroughly brainwashed by Heathcliff—replies that he'd prefer having her as his wife since people always love their wives and husbands better than anyone else. Cathy unwisely disagrees, pointing out that his own parents, from what she's heard, did not get on so famously. Linton, knowing, of course, nothing of the history of Isabella and Heathcliff, becomes enraged, and the two end up quarreling violently. Cathy accuses Linton's father of being "a wicked man," and Linton accuses Cathy's of being "a sneaking fool." Finally, Cathy gives Linton's chair a furious push and the weak boy is seized by a suffocating cough. After he recovers, Cathy, feeling rather guilty, does her best to apologize and make him comfortable. She reads to him and props him up with pillows until it's time to leave.

As the two make their farewells, Linton tries to elicit a promise from Cathy that she will come again the next day. Nelly replies that her charge cannot return. However, just before leaving, Cathy whispers something to Linton which seems to relieve his anxiety on that score. Once outside, Nelly is worried. She warns Cathy not to plan another visit. In any case, she says, Linton is not worth the girl's trouble, being "the worst-tempered bit of a sickly slip that ever struggled into its teens." Cathy declares that Linton would recover quickly enough from his illness if he had her to help care for him. Nelly replies that, Linton will never survive, no matter what kind of coddling he gets. In any case, she categorically forbids Cathy to see him again and threatens to inform Edgar of any such attempt on his daughter's part. Cathy's only answer to this is a sullen "We'll see."

When the pair reach home, Edgar, imagining that they have gone for their usual stroll, does not ask them to explain their absence. Nelly, thoroughly soaked from the wet journey, almost immediately comes down with a bad cold. She is confined to her bed for three weeks, the first time an illness has ever made her unfit to perform her duties. During this time, Cathy divides her days between Nelly and Edgar, so that Nelly, suspecting nothing, never considers what the girl does with herself after tea. And though Cathy often has "a fresh colour in her checks" when she looks in to bid Nelly good night, the faithful servant imagines it is the result of "a hot fire in the library" rather than "a cold ride across the moors."

COMMENT

The quarrel which Catherine and Linton have over the lives of their parents is a dramatic representation of how the first generation of the novel continues to influence the second generation. Still, the way in which the cards, so to speak, have all been shuffled and dealt again—the same cards but in different arrangements—helps to prepare the reader for a new ending to the story the second time around. The chapter is also notable for another reason. Nelly Dean's convenient and unprecedented three-week illness, which permits Cathy to make secret visits to the Heights, is one of the few occasions in the book when Emily Brontë seems to fairly blatantly manipulate her characters for the sake of the plot.

CHAPTER 24

After three weeks of illness, Nelly is able to return to some of her household duties. On her first night up, she asks Cathy to read to her since her eyes are weak. The girl, usually so cooperative, seems strangely unwilling, though eventually she complies. She displays the same odd behavior on subsequent evenings—pleading fatigue or headaches to retire early. On the third night Nelly becomes suspicious and she discovers Cathy returning from Wuthering Heights on her pony. Determined to get to the bottom of the matter, the servant cross-examines her young mistress and finds that Cathy actually has visited the Heights every evening for the last three weeks.

Her secret out, Cathy now gives Nelly an account of the events of these days. Her first visit was managed with the help of a stableboy, Michael, whom she bribed with books, since he was fond of reading, and he then continued to help her all along. On her second visit, she says, Hareton and Joseph were out, so she and Linton had the place more or less to themselves. Zillah, the housekeeper, brought them wine and gingerbread, and the cousins laughed and chatted merrily as they curled up before the hearth. Their only disagreement was about how they would spend an ideal summer's day. Linton—with his languid, invalid's nature—dreamed of lying from dawn till dusk "on a bank of heath in the middle of the moors." Cathy on the other hand—with her health and high spirits—longed for "all to sparkle and dance in a glorious jubilee." She thought Linton's fantasy of "an ecstasy of peace" only "half alive," and he thought her heaven would be "drunk." The pair "began to grow snappish," but at last they kissed and made up, agreeing to try both ways as soon as the right weather came. Later, after they played some games and sang songs, Cathy went "flying home, light as air; and I dreamt of Wuthering Heights, and my sweet darling cousin til morning."

Her next visit began badly. She encountered Hareton at the door, who elatedly declared that he could now read the inscription over the entryway. To prove it, he carefully pronounced the syllables of "Hareton Earnshaw"—but Cathy, unimpressed, called him "a dunce" when he couldn't read the numbers in the date, too. Reddening, he skulked off, a picture of mortified vanity.

Inside, Cathy found Linton lying on the sofa. He complained that he was ill and asked her to read to him. Just as she was about to begin, Hareton—who must have been brooding on the earlier insult—burst in and, in a voice choked with passion, ordered Linton to his room. Then, without giving the boy a chance to reply, he shoved him out into the kitchen, with Cathy following, and barred the door.

Linton was thrown into a rage by this and, shrieking that he would kill Hareton, fell to the ground in a fit of helpless fury, with blood gushing from his mouth. Cathy ran to get Zillah, who took the prostrate patient upstairs with Hareton's help, as Joseph, watching, declared sourly that "the father," Heathcliff, was "thear" in Linton after all!

Later on, as Cathy was riding home, Hareton, now penitent, stepped out of the shadows by the road and tried to apologize. "I gave him a cut with my whip," the unsympathetic girl reports, "and he let go, thundering one of his horrid curses." For the next two days she was too frightened by what she had seen to attempt a return visit to the Heights, even though she actually feared for her cousin's life.

Finally, on the third day, she took courage and stole off again to see Linton. She found him "mending nicely" in a little parlor, but he would not talk to her, blaming the whole uproar on her rather than on Hareton. Infuriated, she left at once. The following day, still angry, she stayed home again, but the day after that her resolution melted, she informs Nelly, and she set out again on Minny.

This time she found Linton himself apologetic. In a solemn tone he begged her to understand and forgive his defects, explaining that when he believes his father's talk of his worthlessness is true, it makes him feel "so cross and bitter, I hate everybody." But, he adds, if only he could be "as sweet, and as kind, and as good" as Cathy, he would be. "Your kindness has made me love you deeper than if I deserved your love," he tells his cousin, and on this note the two are reconciled, but weepingly—for Cathy pities Linton's "distorted nature."

Since that night, Cathy goes on, she regularly visited the boy in his little parlor, but the cousins are rarely merry any more: their visits now are usually rather dreary and troubled. As for Heathcliff, Cathy thinks he deliberately avoids her, and she begs Nelly to let her continue her visits without telling her father and upsetting his peace of mind. Nelly promises to think the matter over. But despite Cathy's pleas, the servant feels obliged to inform her master at once of his daughter's activities. Alarmed and distressed, Edgar forbids any future trips to Wuthering Heights. Cathy weeps and pleads, but the only comfort he will give is a promise to allow Linton to visit her at the Grange as often as he likes. Had he known of the boy's selfish disposition and poor health, Nelly adds, he might have withheld "even that slight consolation."

COMMENT

The triangular relationship which had once involved Heathcliff and Edgar and Catherine so painfully in one another's lives now begins to emerge in the second generation. Hareton has grown somewhat fond of Cathy, though he can express his affection only clumsily, and his jealousy of Linton only with violence. The pride he takes in being able to read his name cut into the stone over the entrance to the Heights is touching, and beyond that, suggests metaphorically that in the presence of Cathy he is beginning to come into his birthright—Wuthering Heights, of course, but more importantly, love.

The conversation which Linton and Cathy have about how each would spend a hot July day expresses more directly than anything else in the novel the two opposing ways of life represented by Thrushcross Grange and Wuthering Heights. Linton's desire for peace and Cathy's longing for sparkle and dance suggest the contrast of calm and storm which one critic has suggested lies at the heart of the book.

CHAPTER 25

"These things happened last winter, Sir," Nelly tells Lockwood, "less than a year ago." Little did she guess then she might soon be amusing a stranger with these stories. "Yet who knows how long you'll be a stranger?" she remarks to Lockwood, hinting that perhaps his interest in Cathy will prove to be a romantic one, since he has even asked to have the girl's picture hung above the fireplace at the Grange. Lockwood replies that he doubts Cathy could return any affection he might have for her, and that besides, he must soon return to his own "busy world." But he begs her to continue her story anyway.

Cathy obeyed her father's commands, Nelly continues, because her affection for him was at this time the chief sentiment in her heart. As his health declines, however, Edgar himself becomes concerned about his daughter's future and begins to wonder if the match with Linton might not be a good one after all. Nelly informs him that if Miss Cathy had the misfortune to marry her cousin, "he would not be beyond her control, unless she were extremely and foolishly indulgent." As the two converse in this way, on a misty February afternoon, Edgar confides to Nelly that he feels his death to be approaching. He has been very happy with his little Cathy, he tells the servant, but on the other hand he is always yearning, too, to rejoin his dead wife. If he could only believe that Linton—in spite of being Heathcliff's son—could take his own place in the girl's heart, he would die peacefully. But if Linton should be unworthy, he adds, "I'd rather resign her to God, and lay her in the earth before me." Without directly giving her opinion of Cathy's cousin, Nelly promises staunchly to be the girl's "friend and counsellor to the last" and assures Edgar that his daughter is a good girl who will be rewarded by life in the end.

The next spring, on Cathy's seventeenth birthday, Edgar decides to "defer" his visit to the churchyard. To Nelly's experienced eyes, he is now so ill that his next "visit" is bound to be a permanent one. Worried about his daughter, he writes again to Linton, asking to see him, but the boy is himself too sick to venture so far, and he is instructed by his father to beg Edgar to "meet him, sometimes, on his rambles," on the moor. Furthermore, he goes on to declare that his health is better, but "while I remain cut off from all hope, and doomed to solitude . . . how can I be cheerful and well?" Edgar is sorry for the boy, but cannot let Cathy meet him alone and is himself not well enough to leave the Grange. He promises, however, to try to see him sometime during the summer and meanwhile suggests he write often.

Linton keeps in touch with Edgar by letter now and, Nelly notes, "had he been unrestrained would probably have spoiled all by filling his epistles with complaints and lamentations, but his father kept a sharp watch over him," so that he writes instead only of the hardship of being separated from Cathy. Cathy herself is a "powerful ally" at the Grange, and between them they persuade Edgar to let them have a ride or a walk together under Nelly's surveillance on the moors nearest the Grange. One reason Edgar is so willing to allow this is that his health is still declining in June, and he cannot leave the house. Another reason is that "he had a natural desire" that Cathy might "retain, or, at least, return in a short time, to the house of her ancestors"—and the only way to do this is to marry Linton, his heir. He had no idea, reflects Nelly, "that the latter was failing almost as fast as he"—and that Heathcliff, who treated his dying son with unnatural cruelty, was himself scheming to achieve a match between the young people for his own wicked reasons.

COMMENT

Nelly and Lockwood continue to suggest how their understanding of the real situation at the Heights is limited. While the housekeeper archly suggests that the tenant of Thrushcross Grange, because of his evident interest in the young Cathy, may not much longer be a stranger in the neighborhood, Lockwood blandly dismisses the idea of such a grotesque match. Although he feels the match would not be impossible, his dismissal is based on the grounds that such a marriage might disturb his tranquility. This passage is one more warning that we must not take all of the narrator's comments at their face value. As for Linton's rapid decline, we may see in the fading of Heathcliff's son the great weakness in the father's plan for revenge. Let him plan and scheme and rage all he wants, the future stands before him in the persons of Cathy and Hareton—no part of his own stock—and before the vitality of that future he will very shortly have to withdraw.

CHAPTER 26

Summer is already past its prime when Cathy and Nelly set out on their first ride to join her cousin. It is a close sultry day, and when they arrive at the appointed spot, they find only a little herd-boy, who tells them that "Master Linton" is waiting for them further on, near the Heights. Nelly is annoyed, but the two travel on till they find the boy, within a quarter of a mile of the farmhouse. He looks so sick and weak that even Nelly is shocked, and Cathy herself is gravely alarmed. She asks him if he isn't worse than usual, and Nelly exclaims that surely he isn't in fit health for rambling on the moors. The young invalid, however, obviously in mortal fear of his father, assures them desperately that he is "better," and when his visitors propose to depart—after half an hour of desultory and depressing conversation—Linton frantically begs them to remain another half-hour at least. He asks Cathy, moreover, to tell her uncle that he is "in tolerable health" and to agree to meet him again the next Thursday.

Cathy is bewildered by all this, but Nelly guesses that Heathcliff has moved on from passive to active hatred of Linton, and that the boy is suffering much abuse at his father's hands. She cannot explain this to Cathy, however, who wonders in annoyed confusion "Why did he wish to see me? . . . In his crossest humours, formerly, I liked him better than I do in his present curious mood. It's just as if it were a task he was compelled to perform—this interview—for fear his father should scold him." But she herself, she continues, has no fear to Heathcliff!

A moment later, Linton, who had fallen asleep from illness and exhaustion, wakes trembling and imagining that he has heard his father's voice. Nelly and Cathy assure him that no one is there but the three of them, and he bursts into tears. Within another minute, however, Heathcliff himself actually does approach. Cathy and Nelly hurry away quickly, promising to return the next Thursday. By the time the pair reach home, Nelly reports, Cathy's annoyance has softened into "a perplexed sensation of pity and regret." Nelly, too, is doubtful about Linton's "actual circumstances," and when they are questioned by Edgar, neither reveals very much of what happened on the moors. As Nelly puts it, "I hardly knew what to hide, and what to reveal."

COMMENT

It is plain now that Linton is dying and that his father is using him in a last, desperate bid for revenge. Perhaps Cathy might have noticed all this too if her genuinely affectionate nature had not made her concentrate all her attention on the boy's immediate sorrow and pain.

Whatever Nelly may know of the matter cannot be conveyed to the ailing Edgar, and so the stage is set for the violence of the next chapter.

CHAPTER 27

Seven more days "glide" past and now Edgar Linton's state grows rapidly worse. There is no longer any possibility of keeping Cathy from the fact that her father is dying. When Thursday arrives, she does not even have the heart to mention her appointment with Linton—and when her father and Nelly give her permission to ride out to meet him, she is reluctant to leave Edgar's side. Her father, however, has a fixed idea that "as his nephew resembled him in person, he would resemble him in mind," and Nelly, anxious not to disturb his last moments, refrains from disillusioning him. Thus, in accordance with his wishes, Cathy and her old nurse set out to see her cousin that very afternoon.

They find Linton at the same spot where they had seen him the previous week. He seems as sick as he did then, too, and if anything, even more terrified of Heathcliff's displeasure. Since he displays little enough fondness for his cousin, Cathy—who cannot sympathize with his plight—angrily demands to know why he has brought her from her father's bedside. Linton humbly begs the girl not to be angry with him but to try to understand his fears. "I'm too mean for your anger," he declares. "Hate my father, and spare me, for contempt." Cathy is even more scornful of this but, "convulsed with exquisite terror," her cousin throws himself on the ground, sobbing "Catherine, Catherine, I'm a traitor too, and I dare not tell! But leave me and I shall be killed!"

Cathy and Nelly are baffled by this mysterious speech. But the girl asserts that she is not afraid of Heathcliff and the two remain, trying to comfort the anguished Linton as best they can. In another moment Heathcliff himself appears on the scene. Ignoring the young people, he asks Nelly in an undertone if her master is in fact dying, and she answers that he is. Next he inquires about his son's behavior. "Is he pretty lively with Miss Linton generally?" But Nelly replies that the boy should be in bed, under a doctor's care. "He shall be in a day or two," mutters Heathcliff. Then, turning to Linton, he snarls, "Get up! Don't grovel on the ground there—up this moment!" The sick boy is barely able to stand, but his father drags him to his feet anyway and asks Cathy to assist him in getting the invalid home. She explains that she is forbidden to go to Wuthering Heights, but Linton "implores her to accompany him, with a frantic importunity that admitted no denial."

Nelly disapproves but cannot stop the girl, and soon the whole group has arrived at the Heights. Once inside, Heathcliff shuts and locks the door. He informs them that Hareton, Joseph and Zillah are all away for the time being, and the girl and her nurse quickly realize that they are now the treacherous man's prisoners. When Cathy tries to seize the key from him, he grabs it away and beats her violently about the head. Nelly tries to come to the girl's rescue, but is hurled aside with a savage blow to the chest. Cathy is bewildered by this mad violence and trembles like a reed. Heathcliff grimly tells her to "Go to Linton now . . . and cry at your ease! I shall be your father tomorrow—all the father you'll have in a few days . . ." With these and a few other brutal words, he goes out to get the horses which Nelly and her mistress left on the moor.

While he is gone, the two try to force open a door but are unable to escape. They then question Linton who, no longer in fear of his father now that he has accomplished the man's diabolical purpose, displays his true selfishness by remaining hatefully composed. "Papa wants us to be married," he admits, "and he knows your papa wouldn't let us marry now; and he's afraid of my dying, if we wait; so we are to be married in the morning, and you are to stay here all night, and if you do as he wishes, you shall return home next day and take me with you." But Cathy's only reaction to this is a desperate resolve to escape in light of the distress such an absence will surely cause her father. Linton, fearful that he may be blamed if the plan fails, resumes his usual weeping and moaning, and is thus occupied when the "jailer," Heathcliff, returns.

After Linton has been sent to bed, Cathy pleads with Heathcliff to let her return to the Grange. She notes that her father will be miserable and she cannot endure the thought of him suffering so in his last days. Heathcliff answers spitefully that "I shall enjoy myself remarkably in thinking your father will be miserable," and goes on to add that, in any case, "his happiest days were over when your days began." Furthermore, when Cathy begs pitifully to be allowed to leave, declaring that she'll marry Linton within the hour if only she can be back at home by nightfall, Heathcliff's only reply is to "brutally repulse her . . . as if his flesh crept in aversion."

Nelly and Cathy sit weeping with frustration until about nine o'clock, when they are sent to spend the night in Zillah's room. Neither can sleep, however, and they spend a dismal night, Cathy anxiously seated by the window and Nelly rocking back and forth on a chair, blaming herself for the whole misfortune. At seven in the morning, Heathcliff comes and pulls Cathy out of the room, but Nelly is forced to remain within. In fact, the housekeeper is imprisoned in this little room for five more nights and four more days. She sees only Hareton, who brings her food—"and he was a model of a jailer—surly, and dumb, and deaf to every attempt at moving his sense of justice or compassion."

COMMENT

Heathcliff, who has seldom before resorted to a specifically illegal act to achieve his goal, now stoops to kidnapping Cathy and Nelly. His recklessness is a sign of his desperation. The laws of inheritance are complex and his situation has suddenly become critical. Should Linton die before he can marry Cathy, all will be lost.

On the other hand, even if the marriage takes place, Heathcliff cannot be sure of success unless Edgar dies before Linton. With both the boy and the man on the very brink of death, every moment is precious, and for Heathcliff the end clearly justifies the means.

CHAPTER 28

After Nelly has spent five days in her jail, Zillah arrives with word that Nelly and Cathy are rumored in Gimmerton to have been lost in the Blackhorse marsh. Heathcliff, amused, allows his housekeeper to see Nelly, explaining that "the bog water got into her head . . . but she's now well enough to leave and go home." Tell her, he adds to Zillah, that "her young lady will follow in time to attend the Squire's funeral." Alarmed, Nelly asks if her master is dead, but Zillah replies that Dr. Kenneth, whom she's just met on the road, thinks he may last another day.

Free at last, Nelly rushes downstairs, anxiously seeking Cathy. The only person in sight is Linton, lying on the sofa sucking a stick of sugar candy. When Nelly questions him about Cathy's whereabouts, he replies apathetically that "she's upstairs—she's not to go." His father has told him, he adds, "not to be soft with Catherine—she's my wife, and it's shameful that she should wish to leave me! He says she hates me, and wants me to die, that she may have my money, but she shan't have it, and she shan't go home!" Shocked, Nelly reminds Linton of Cathy's many kindnesses to him, but he is barely moved. "She cries so I can't bear it," he complains. He adds that she had tried to bribe him to help her escape by promising him her pretty things, her books, her pony, and even her locket with the pictures of her parents. But he had told her they were all his anyway, and when she began to fight with him over the locket, Heathcliff himself had intervened and taken it from her, keeping the portrait of her mother and crushing the one of her father with his foot. Then he hit Cathy again across the mouth and, Linton concludes, since then the girl has not spoken to him, but "looks so pale and wild I'm afraid of her."

Nelly tries to get the boy to talk more, hoping he'll reveal the whereabouts of the key to the room in which Cathy is locked. But he guesses her intention, and turning his face away, cries "I shan't tell you where it is! It is our secret." Under the circumstances, Nelly considers it best to give up and send a rescue party for the girl from the Grange. She hurries home and once there rushes immediately to Edgar's bedside, without stopping to satisfy the curiosity of her fellow servants.

She finds the master of Thrushcross Grange much changed even in these few days. Sad and resigned, he is waiting for death—but somehow he looks even younger than his thirty-nine years. When he murmurs Cathy's name, Nelly informs him gently that his daughter is coming soon and is alive and well. At this, he sinks momentarily into a swoon from the shock of the news. When he recovers, Nelly tells him of their "compulsory visit and detention at the Heights," softening the harsh facts as much as possible so as not to upset him unduly. He quickly realizes that one of his enemy's objects is "to secure the personal property as well as the estate to his son, or rather himself," and therefore decides that his will needs to be changed so that Cathy's fortune is left in the hands of trustees in order that Heathcliff cannot get hold of it.

Nelly sends a man to fetch Mr. Green, the lawyer, and a party of four strong men to rescue Cathy from the Heights. The first man, however, returns after several hours with word that the lawyer has business in the village but will try to get to the Grange before morning. The rescue party, too, returns without completing its mission, having been told by the devious Heathcliff that Cathy was too ill to leave her room. Cursing their stupidity, Nelly resolves to lead a posse to the Heights herself at daylight.

As she goes downstairs at three in the morning, however, the housekeeper hears a frantic knock at the door. Answering, she discovers Cathy, pale and wild after a hazardous escape from her prison. Without staying for an explanation, Nelly washes the girl's face and leads her to her father's bedside, where the two are reunited just in time. Cathy remains calm as her father dies blissfully, glad to see his daughter safely home, and radiant at the thought of being with his long-dead wife after so many years of separation. "I am going to her," he murmurs at the last, "and you, darling child, shall come to us."

At dinnertime, the lawyer finally appears. He had apparently been in Heathcliff's employ, which was why he didn't answer Edgar's summons sooner. Now he takes it upon himself to order everybody around. All the servants but Nelly are dismissed, and he tries to insist on Edgar being buried in the chapel with his family rather than outside with his wife; but Nelly, supported by her master's will, is able at least to prevent that.

After the funeral, Cathy and Nelly are allowed to remain at the Grange temporarily. When the two are alone again, Cathy tells her nurse about her escape from Wuthering Heights. Evidently her anguish had "at last spurred Linton to incur the risk of liberating her"—not because of any compassion for her, however, but because her furious desperation terrified him. He tried hard to dissociate himself from her actions. He pretended to lock the door without actually shutting it and slept in Hareton's room afterwards. But, Nelly says, he suffered for his share in the escape, despite "his timid contrivances."

COMMENT

Edgar dies without having changed his will. All his property goes to his daughter and her husband, and because Heathcliff has forced Linton to make him his heir, only one more precarious life stands between the master of Wuthering Heights and the fulfillment of his revenge. It is not by chance that Edgar fails in his attempt to alter his will. Heathcliff has bought off the local lawyer, and has, in short, spread his infection of hate through the whole countryside. Now more than ever the reader understands how necessary it is for the "illness" at Wuthering Heights be cured, and that love and life be substituted for hatred and death.

CHAPTER 29

On the night of her father's funeral, Cathy sits with Nelly in the library at Thrushcross Grange. The two agree that Cathy might try to get permission to stay on at the Grange as long as Linton is alive, keeping Nelly as housekeeper. At just this moment Heathcliff is announced. He steps once more into the room he has not seen for eighteen years. Paintings of Catherine and Edgar look down on a Heathcliff to whom, a stranger would have said, the years had been kind. He has grown only a little heavier, and if his face is paler now than it was, it is also more composed.

Heathcliff has come to call Cathy back to the Grange. Linton needs tending and his father, having gotten all the use he can from him, no longer wants to be bothered with the sickly boy. As for the suggestion that Linton and Cathy live together at the Grange, Heathcliff announces that he is seeking a tenant for the place and that, in any case, he wants his children about him. He orders Cathy to get busy packing her things, warning her not to expect to find her husband in a very good temper. He is angry with her for having left him, and beyond that, has been reduced to despair by a new torture which Heathcliff has devised. The torture consists simply of the father forcing his son to sit in his presence for two hours.

When Cathy has gone, Heathcliff tells Nelly that he wants Catherine's portrait delivered to the Heights. Not that he needs a picture of her, he says, for only yesterday he had gotten the sexton, who was digging Edgar's grave, to open Catherine's grave as well, and he had stared for a long time at the only slightly altered and still beloved face. Then he had broken open the side of her coffin—the side away from Edgar—and had bribed the sexton to open the side of his coffin (set aside for Heathcliff's eventual burial) so that the two lovers might lie together in the grave, mingling their substance until men could no longer say which was which.

For eighteen years, he continues, he has been haunted by Catherine. On the night of her funeral he had been on the point of digging her up and taking her in his arms once more. Then he had heard a sigh above him in the stormy churchyard, a sigh often repeated, which had assured him that Catherine's spirit was there in the air and not in the ground. He had hurried home that night, the night of the battle with Hindley, and climbing to his room, had felt more strongly than ever the presence of Catherine's spirit. Heathcliff says that he believes in ghosts and that for eighteen years Catherine's ghost has disturbed him, "night and day, incessantly, remorselessly." The sight of her the night before, however, had restored him to a certain tranquility, and he had dreamed that he was sleeping the last sleep by the sleeper, with his heart stopped and his cheek frozen against hers.

At this moment, the second Cathy returns to the library, and as she is preparing to leave, she asks Nelly to visit her often at the Heights. "Take care you do no such thing," says Heathcliff, "I want none of your prying at my house." And with that, he hurries the girl away.

COMMENT

This is one of the chapters in which Emily Brontë invites our sympathy for Heathcliff. The profundity of the man's feeling and the extent of his torment cannot fail to touch us, even if his description of his life seems to be one protracted snarl. Here, too, for the first time, we have an explanation of Heathcliff's wild reply to Lockwood's indiscreet remark: "Oh, you would intimate that her spirit has taken the post of ministering angel, and guards the fortunes of Wuthering Heights, even when her body is gone." This remark, which gave rise to Lockwood's nightmare and Heathcliff's violent reaction to it, plainly illustrates Heathcliff's conviction that for many years he has been haunted by Catherine's ghost. And his desire that in death their two bodies should be mingled together seems to substantiate Catherine's statement: "He is more myself than I am."

CHAPTER 30

Nelly does not see Cathy again after the night of Edgar's funeral. Once she goes to the Heights, but Joseph will not open the door to her. She does encounter Zillah on the moor one day, however, shortly before Lockwood's arrival, and from the "narrow-minded, selfish woman" learns what has been going on at the Heights since Cathy has been living there.

On the first night, Cathy had gone directly to Linton without greeting anyone. She remained in his room until morning, when she came down to inform Heathcliff that Linton was very ill and needed a doctor. Heathcliff replied that he knew it but that, because Linton wasn't worth a farthing, not a farthing would be spent on him for medical aid.

Cathy at first seeks the help of Zillah in caring for her sick husband, but Zillah refuses to disobey her master's orders that no one but Cathy should attend Linton. In fact, Zillah makes a great point of what a proper servant she is. Though she sees that Linton's death is being hastened by Heathcliff's refusal to send for a doctor, she does nothing to help him on the grounds that a good servant never meddles in her master's affairs. "It was," she concludes primly, "no concern of mine."

Cathy must make do as best she can, and her best cannot save Linton. One night she awakens the house with the cry that Linton is dying, and by the time Heathcliff, cursing all the while, reaches his son's bed, the boy is dead. For the next two weeks, Cathy keeps to her room, where she is visited only once by Heathcliff. He comes to show the girl his son's will. The will was written when Linton was sick and under pressure from his father, leaving all of the moveable property of Thrushcross Grange—Cathy's inheritance, of course, but legally her husband's to dispose of—to Heathcliff. Linton, being a minor, could not meddle with the lands, but these Heathcliff claims through his wife, Isabella. Thus, Cathy is without money or friends, and Heathcliff is at last the master of Wuthering Heights and Thrushcross Grange.

The cold finally forces Cathy to leave her room one Sunday. Heathcliff has ridden off to the Grange, and only Hareton and Zillah are downstairs. Hareton displays real eagerness when he hears that Cathy will join them, and in his lumpish way he tries to be helpful. He even gets some books for the girl from a shelf that is too high for her to reach, and sits beside her while she reads. But when he goes so far as to touch one of her curls, he is violently rebuffed. Still, he whispers to Zillah to ask Cathy to read to them. When the girl refuses, saying that because they did nothing to help her in her days of need, she will do nothing for them, Hareton—protesting that he had offered to help—subsides again into his usual sullenness.

From that day, Zillah concludes in her account to Nelly, though Cathy has been forced to remain with the other inhabitants of the Heights, she has had no "lover or liker" among them. She snaps at everyone and even dares Heathcliff to thrash her, for the more hurt she gets the more venomous she grows. Only a new marriage will rescue her from that house, Nelly says a bit pointedly to Lockwood, as she brings her narrative to a close, "and that scheme it does not come within my province to arrange."

For his part, Lockwood has been recovering somewhat more quickly than expected and proposes to ride over to the Heights to tell Heathcliff that he will be spending the next six months in London. The following summer he will return to the Grange but does not plan to spend another winter in the neighborhood.

COMMENT

Most significant for the future history of the Heights is the suggestion of Hareton's feelings of tenderness for Cathy. True, in this chapter we see them being rebuffed, and we are aware that Heathcliff stands ready to crush any possibility of healthy love between the two, just as Hindley had destroyed that possibility for Heathcliff and Catherine. Still, we have a sense here of the direction in which matters may yet move.

CHAPTER 31

Lockwood sets off for the Heights carrying a note from Nelly Dean to Cathy. As at his last visit, he finds the gate locked and has to "invoke" Hareton to open it and let him in. Hareton, the visitor remarks snidely, is a handsome rustic who apparently does his best to make the least of his advantages. Heathcliff is not due home until dinnertime and Lockwood decides to wait. He drifts over to a window beside which Cathy is sitting, and under the pretense of desiring a view of the garden, he drops Nelly's note into the girl's lap.

With her usual petulance, Cathy sweeps the note from her skirts, much embarrassing Lockwood, whose little subterfuge has been uncovered and who is further displeased at the thought that the girl's violent reaction signifies her belief in his authorship of the note. The girl, Lockwood thinks, looks more sulky and less spirited than before. She's a beauty, to be sure, he decides, but not an angel.

Meanwhile, Hareton, having watched the byplay with the note, snatches it up, puts it in his pocket, and promises to show it to Heathcliff. But as Cathy turns her head away and begins to cry, the boy relents and flings the message at her feet as ungraciously as he can. Cathy devours Nelly's words and then begins to think back over her happy times at the Grange. In her melancholy musing she reveals, much to Lockwood's dismay, that she does not have even a single book for a companion at the Heights. Heathcliff has destroyed most of her small library, she says, and the few volumes that remained to her were stolen by Hareton, no doubt because, being ignorant himself, he could not bear the thought of anyone else taking pleasure from books.

At this, Hareton bridles, for as it soon becomes clear, he has taken the books not to deprive Cathy of her pleasure but rather to try to learn to do, himself, the things that please her. Lockwood understands this, but Catherine either cannot or will not. "He has selected my favorite pieces to recite and mutilate," she complains, "as if out of deliberate malice!" But the reader can easily see that Hareton's choice of selections to memorize is dictated by a feeling very different from malice.

Angry now, Hareton leaves the room and returns shortly with the half-dozen volumes he has taken from Cathy and from which he has been studying with such comical determination. He tosses them into the girl's lap, announcing that he never wants to see them again, and Cathy, for her part, flings them to the floor, saying that she cannot bear the thought of reading books connected with him, and embarking on a cruel imitation of the boy's painful attempts of reading. Hareton finally loses control of himself and strikes Cathy, an act of which Lockwood finds himself approving, and then, in an anguished "sacrifice to spleen," throws onto the fire the books from which he had hoped to learn how to please Cathy.

At this moment, a leaner and moodier Heathcliff than Lockwood had seen six weeks before enters and, catching sight of the departing Hareton, begins to mutter to himself about how much like the older Catherine the boy is growing to look. "I can hardly bear to see him," he says, and wonders if that face will not finally lead him to abandon his obsessive quest for revenge.

Noticing Lockwood and learning of his tenant's plans to depart for London, Heathcliff cannot resist insulting the man by asking him if he has come to beg off paying his rent. Lockwood reacts by offering to pay the amount in full at once, but Heathcliff coolly refuses to take the money and, instead, invites his tenant to stay for dinner. Cathy is banished to the kitchen to eat with Joseph, leading Lockwood to speculate that after all she is probably incapable of appreciating a better class of people when she meets them. The meal is a cheerless one and the guest soon leaves the Heights, thinking smugly to himself, as he proceeds home, how fortunate Cathy might have been had he, Lockwood, grown attached to her and borne her off into the stirring atmosphere of the town.

COMMENT

Once again the reader is in the hands of the obtuse Lockwood and once again, in order to learn what is going on at the Heights, we must read between the lines of the narrative. It is, however, an easy enough job to see through Lockwood's smugness and self-satisfaction to the possibility of real affection between Hareton and Cathy, and to the waning of Heathcliff's own power and influence. Heathcliff's remark on catching sight of Hareton—"It will be odd if I thwart myself"—signals the beginning of the end of the man's agony in this world.

CHAPTER 32

In September 1802, Lockwood finds himself once more in the neighborhood of Gimmerton. He decides to spend the night at Thrushcross Grange where, to his surprise, he learns that Ellen Dean has moved to Wuthering Heights. Wondering what the change can mean, he sets out to visit Nelly, leaving the new housekeeper, agitated at the sudden appearance of her master, to make some supper, lay a fire, and prepare a bed.

On his way, Lockwood notes the setting sun and the rising moon—the one fading and the other brightening. As he reaches the Heights, he is amazed to see the front gate unlocked and to smell the fragrance of flowers in the yard. Through a window he catches sight of Cathy and Hareton, seated together over a book, the girl teaching the boy and the boy claiming kisses as rewards for his aptness. As the couple start out of the house for one of their long, nightly rambles, Lockwood correctly surmises that he would only be in the way, and hurries around to the kitchen. He finds Joseph sitting and complaining in his usual self-righteous way, and he encounters Nelly. She is surprised and happy to see him, explaining that she had been brought from the Grange to the Heights by Heathcliff on the departure of Zillah. When Lockwood broaches the subject of his rent, Nelly tells him he must take the matter up with Cathy, as Mr. Heathcliff is dead. Astonished, Lockwood asks Nelly to continue her story of Heathcliff, and to account for his "queer end."

On her return to the Heights, Nelly says, she was shocked to see the alteration in Cathy's appearance. Following Heathcliff's orders, she kept the girl out of sight, but more and more Cathy seemed to want to go to the kitchen to argue with Hareton. The reason soon became plain. She was ashamed of the way she had discouraged his attempts at self-improvement, and her abuse of the boy now was only a disguise for her growing affection. Hareton gradually allowed his hurt feelings to be mollified, but soon enough he was permitting Cathy to teach him to read, and as his mind awakened, the sullen cloud lifted from his face. The transformation was not an overnight one, of course. Hareton cannot be "civilized with a wish," nor is Cathy a "paragon of patience." But both have the same goal, and so both persevere. Now things have gone far enough for Nelly to anticipate their wedding day, a day on which there will not be a happier woman than herself in all England.

COMMENT

As Lockwood approaches Wuthering Heights, he sees the setting sun and the rising moon—"the one fading and the other brightening." These celestial sights are obvious symbols of the changing of the guard at the Heights. Then, for the first time in Lockwood's experience, the gate is open to the house on the hill and perfume of flowers grace the yard. The reader hardly needs to be told that Heathcliff is dead. The return of life and sanity to the Heights proclaims this fact. Only old Joseph, his zealot's fury now a mockery of itself, remains as a link to the past.

CHAPTER 33

Nelly continues her narrative of Heathcliff's last days. Hareton is recovering from the effects of a shooting accident and cannot do any heavy work. He is performing some light tasks in the garden when Cathy convinces him to help her remove the gooseberry and currant bushes that grow there in order to make room for some flowers she plans to import from the Grange. The plan horrifies Nelly, who knows that the blackcurrant trees are special favorites of old Joseph's.

Before breakfast, Nelly warns Cathy not to show her affection for Hareton too openly before Heathcliff. However, no sooner is the household seated at the table than the girl begins to tease her cousin by putting primroses in his porridge. Heathcliff, roused from a reverie by the sounds of giggling, turns on the pair and angrily cries, "I thought I had cured you of laughing." A few moments later, Joseph bursts into the room, complaining bitterly about his currant-trees. Cathy confesses her part in the scheme and then goes on to taunt Heathcliff, saying that he should not begrudge her and Hareton a few square yards of ground, since he has stolen all of their land and money.

Furious, Heathcliff leaps at the girl, who warns him that Hareton will take her side in any argument. Hareton does indeed take Cathy's part, though it is plain that he feels torn between two obligations. Suddenly, Heathcliff relents. He warns Cathy not to put him in such a passion again, lest he murder her, and releases his grip on her hair. Heathcliff then repeats almost word for word the threat which Hindley had years before made to him: Hareton is warned that if he is seen so much as listening to his cousin again, Heathcliff will send him off to seek his bread where he can get it. Heathcliff then remains alone until dinner, after which he leaves the house, indicating that he will be away until evening.

Alone with Hareton, Cathy begins to speak of the blackness of Heathcliff's heart. To her surprise, Hareton refuses to be disloyal to his tormentor, to whom he appears to be attached "by ties stronger than reason would break," and Cathy makes no further effort to come between them. When Heathcliff returns that evening, he finds the two—in spite of his injunction—leaning together over a book. They glance up when he enters, and their eyes seem so uncannily to resemble those of the girl's dead mother that the master of Wuthering Heights is just able to motion them out of the room.

To Nelly, who remains behind, Heathcliff admits that he has lost interest in his scheme of revenge just when it is about to mature. He now has it within his power to destroy both houses, yet he lacks the will to remove one slate from either roof. He feels, he tells Nelly, a strange change approaching. He no longer takes an interest in daily life; he hardly remembers to eat. Only Cathy and Hareton have any reality for him, and he can barely stand to be in their presence. Hareton especially reminds him of himself as a boy, and the two of them, like every other person and object in his life, remind him constantly of the dead Catherine.

When Nelly presses him about the nature of the change he feels approaching, Heathcliff cannot be specific. He does not feel ill and he certainly has no fear of death. Yet he no longer has a desire to live; he has to remind himself to breathe, and everything in his being yearns to attain a single goal. "O God!" he cries, "It is a long fight, I wish it were over."

COMMENT

The collapse of Heathcliff's will to revenge, the main subject of this chapter, is symbolized by the uprooting of Joseph's black-currant trees and the substitution for them of flowers imported from the Grange. Throughout the book, Joseph has been something more than just a comic Yorkshireman. As the spirit of Wuthering Heights, he has constantly invoked the flickering hellfires of his doom-ridden vision, circling the house, as it were, with leaping flames that give no light but bar all life. The removal of the black-currant trees signifies, as Joseph well knows, his own imminent removal by death from the world over which he has so long brooded as the appropriate guardian spirit, and his replacement by Cathy, whose flowers and whose fresh affection his dour nature cannot abide. It is characteristic of this new atmosphere that fanaticism is not able to survive in it. Hareton, who has as much reason to hate Heathcliff as Heathcliff had to hate Hindley, stoutly proclaims his loyalty to the man who sought to destroy him. The old world of the Heights, Joseph's vengeful world, is passing forever.

CHAPTER 34

For some days after his conversation with Nelly, Heathcliff shuns meeting the family at meals; eating once in twenty-four hours seems enough for him. Then one night, when everyone is in bed, Nelly hears him going out through the front door and notices, in the morning, that he has not yet returned. It isn't until after breakfast that he comes in. He is pale and trembling, yet a strange, joyful glitter in his face that changes its whole aspect. Nelly, practical as always, wonders if his night walks and his fasting have not brought on some serious illness or fever. Heathcliff laughs at this idea, but at dinner he is still unable to touch food and stares eagerly toward the window for a while before rising and going out again.

When Hareton hurries after him to see what is wrong, Heathcliff sends him back to Cathy, wondering how he would want the company of anybody else. Later, the agitated man comes inside again, his face still shining with its unnatural appearance of joy. Again he rejects Nelly's offer of food, saying he will wait till supper. "I'm animated with hunger," he explains, "and, seemingly, I must not eat." Nelly pursues the matter, asking Heathcliff where he was the previous night. "On the threshold of hell," he replies, "but today, I am within sight of my heaven. I have my eyes on it—hardly three feet to sever me!"

When at eight o'clock in the evening Heathcliff still has not put in an appearance, Nelly decides to take some food to his room. But the sight of his pale, goblin-like face and dark eyes frightens the housekeeper into dropping her candle. When she sends Joseph up to lay the fire and bring more light, the old man returns with the news that his master is about to retire and will eat nothing until morning. Heathcliff does not, however, spend the night in his own room. Instead, he goes to the room with the panelled bed in which Lockwood had his nightmare. This action prompts Nelly to wonder if the man is some sort of ghoul or vampire. As she recalls the everyday incidents of his childhood and youth, however, she drives these superstitious notions from her mind.

In the morning, Nelly sets breakfast under the trees for Cathy and Hareton and reenters the house to find Heathcliff agitatedly discussing farm business with Joseph. The same excited, joyful expression is on his face. When Joseph leaves, his master takes his usual place at the table and then begins to stare in an uncanny way at a particular spot on the opposite wall, forgetting to breathe for half a minute at a time. When Nelly begs him not to stare so, Heathcliff asks her to turn around and see if they are alone. The housekeeper assures him that they are, but now her master seems to be gazing at something within two yards' distance, something that communicates both pleasure and pain in exquisite extremes. Again Nelly reminds him of his long fast, urging him to eat the food she has kept warm for him. But her entreaties only irritate him and drive him from the house, down the path and through the gate.

Heathcliff returns after midnight and locks himself in the lower room. At four the same morning, Nelly, unable to sleep, goes down to the kitchen, where her activity attracts her master. Once more she urges him to eat, to which he replies that it is not his fault that he cannot eat or rest. He promises to do both as soon as he possibly can, but continues, "You might as well bid a man struggling in the water to rest within arm's length of the shore." He must reach his goal first, he says, and then he will rest. He is too happy and yet not happy enough. The bliss of his soul kills his body but does not satisfy itself.

Nelly is disturbed by this "strange happiness" and urges Heathcliff to send for a minister to learn how unfit he is for heaven. But her talk of heaven and death only reminds Heathcliff of the way in which he wants to be buried. His body must be taken to the churchyard at evening, accompanied by Hareton and Nelly, and the sexton must be reminded of how the two coffins are to be placed together. No minister will be necessary, Heathcliff assures the housekeeper, for he has already attained his heaven, and other people's heavens have no meaning for him. Later in the afternoon he again comes to the kitchen to seek Nelly's company. But Nelly says that she is frightened to be alone with him. Heathcliff replies that there is one who won't shrink from him. "By God, she's relentless," he groans. "Oh, damn it! It's unutterably too much for flesh and blood to bear—even mine."

All that night, Heathcliff groans and mutters to himself. Nelly sends Hareton to get the doctor. When Mr. Kenneth arrives, however, Heathcliff bids him be damned. He's better, he says, and wants to be left alone. The following evening is very wet, as the rain falls until dawn. As Nelly walks around the house, she notices Heathcliff's window swinging open and the rain driving right into his room. She enters the chamber with another key to close the window, naturally assuming that her master is not there. But within the panelled window bed she finds Heathcliff dead, drenched by the long rain of the night.

At the sight of the body, Joseph makes his usual remarks about the devil having carried off Heathcliff's soul, but also notes that the lawful master and the ancient stock have been restored to their rights. Hareton, who has most reason to rejoice at the death, is the only one truly moved by it. He sits sobbing beside the body all night. On the following evening—and to the scandal of the whole neighborhood—Heathcliff is buried in the churchyard as he requested, without the services of a minister (crumbling Gimmerton Church no longer has a minister anyway). Hareton digs green sods from the earth and, weeping bitterly, places them on the grave.

Nelly hopes that the tenant of that grave sleeps soundly, but she has heard disturbing rumors from the country people that Catherine and Heathcliff walk the moors at night and even appear within the house at Wuthering Heights. For this reason she is glad that when Hareton and Catherine marry on New Year's Day, 1803, they will move to the Grange and leave the Heights in the care of old Joseph.

At this moment, the two young lovers return from their walk and Lockwood makes their appearance an excuse for his departure, pressing "a remembrance" into Nelly's hand and setting off for the Grange. On his way home, he passes the old church and seeks out the three headstones on the slope near the moor. Cathy's headstone is half-buried in heath,

Edgar's only harmonized by turf and moss, Heathcliff's still bare.

"I lingered around them," Lockwood says, "under that benign sky; watched the moths fluttering among the heath and harebells; listened to the soft wind breathing through the grass; and wondered how anyone could ever imagine unquiet slumbers for the sleepers in that quiet earth."

COMMENT

This chapter tells of Heathcliff's slow disintegration and death. The death itself is preceded by a fast, reminiscent of the fast which precipitated Catherine's final illness. Heathcliff is described as robust and healthy shortly before his sudden decline. We must conclude that his overwhelming will to die and his desire to return to his beloved Catherine—the thought of which lights his face with a strange joy for days—are responsible for his death. Yet the fast is significant; it is a metaphor for the deprivation which always characterized the relationship of the doomed lovers and which became, therefore, their private language of love. The structure of the book achieves an almost perfect symmetry in the death of Heathcliff. At the end of the novel as at the beginning, the master spirit of Wuthering Heights is staring out into a storm, searching for Catherine.

CHARACTER ANALYSES

HEATHCLIFF

Heathcliff is an extremely complex character. At first glance he may seem entirely wicked, even, at times, a criminal. The vicious way in which he helps to destroy Hindley and brutalizes Isabella and Hareton suggests that he is a man for whom sympathy ought to be impossible. And when he goes so far as to kidnap young Cathy and Nelly Dean, he quite flagrantly breaks the law of society as well at its moral code.

Yet Emily Brontë so manages her dark hero as to make him, at least to a certain extent, a sympathetic figure. Early in the book, for instance, just when it appears that Heathcliff is irrefutably a cruel and insensitive brute, unaware of even the elementary obligation which one human being owes to another—when, in short, he has gone so far as to drive Lockwood out into the storm alone—there comes one of the overwhelmingly lyric moments in the novel as Heathcliff leans far out of the window and implores the spirit of Catherine to come in. The depth of feeling, the compassion of which Heathcliff is plainly capable in this scene, forces us to reconsider our judgment of the man. Without question, he is brutal. However, he just as plainly has within him the potential for great tenderness and great love. Obviously, this potential has been destroyed somewhere along the line, and the reader, piqued to discover how this could have happened, reads on.

In Nelly Dean's narrative we find some explanation for Heathcliff's character. The boy's early years as an orphan in a Liverpool slum no doubt taught him many lessons about the brutality of life, lessons which his next years at Wuthering Heights did little to correct. Still, on the death of old Mr. Earnshaw, he is capable of great sensitivity, comforting Catherine with pictures of heaven more beautiful than a parson could ever imagine.

Heathcliff's real torment, however, is still ahead of him. Just as the perpetual winds which whip the Heights stunt and warp the few trees hardy enough to survive there, so the perpetual hatred of the jealous Hindley twists and thwarts the love in Heathcliff to sullen rage, until, with the desertion of Catherine, all possibility of love disappears forever. Heathcliff, then illustrates perfectly what psychologists and sociologists tell us happens to children who are denied love. They grow incapable of feeling love themselves or pervert it in some destructive way, and a reader would have to be heartless indeed not to commiserate at least a little with a man who has been so cruelly victimized.

Yet no one can read *Wuthering Heights* without feeling that there is more to Heathcliff than a mere sociological case history. He is represented not as someone who hates just in order to fill up the gap made by the withdrawal of love, but as the terrible incarnation of evil, and of evil as a positive force in nature. When we first see him as a boy, he is described as "dark, almost as if came from the devil." Thus, from the beginning the potential for evil exists in the child side by side with the potential for good, and the two equally powerful forces rage within him. In the end, however, it is the force of evil which is victorious.

Indeed, if it were necessary to state the one fact which makes Heathcliff so memorable a character and *Wuthering Heights* so unforgettable a book, that fact would be the way in which Emily Brontë treats darkness and violence as real, positive and inescapable forces in human existence. Heathcliff's whole life is an embodiment of this force of evil. Contemplating his history is like looking at the negative of a favorite photograph; everything that should be dark is light and everything that should be light is dark. Heathcliff and Catherine make love not by giving each other pleasure, but by inflicting one another with great pain. They speak not of living together but of dying together. They sustain themselves not by eating but by refusing to eat. It is Emily Brontë's triumph as a writer that, as the novel proceeds, the negative becomes positive. The perverse love of Catherine and Heathcliff becomes the great reality of the story, and Heathcliff himself, one of the most ferocious creations in literature, finally earns the sympathy and understanding of the careful reader.

CATHERINE EARNSHAW

Catherine Earnshaw is also a complex character. By turns loving and violent, gentle and passionate, affectionate and willful, she is the despair of her father who, because he cannot understand her, says he cannot love her. Where her brother, Hindley, feels dispossessed by Heathcliff, Catherine sees in the dark boy a reflection of her own wild nature and together with him plays on the moors, their natural habitat, absorbing the savage beauty of the countryside.

But Catherine has a fatal weakness. She finds herself irresistibly attracted to the gentility of Thrushcross Grange, to the calm of the lovely old house, so refreshing after the storms of the Heights. Thus, she is led to betray what she herself knows to be her true nature—a nature that is one with Heathcliff's—for the sake of worldly refinement. The tragedy of the novel is precipitated by her decision to marry Edgar since the brutish Heathcliff is socially beneath her. She acknowledges this tragedy in the powerful scene of her reunion with Heathcliff in Chapter 15.

It is on this point that Heathcliff and Catherine differ most markedly, for however cruel, however wicked Heathcliff becomes, he never betrays his dream and his own private vision of himself. Where Catherine seeks a kind of worldly success for its own sake, Heathcliff seeks it only as a way of returning to Catherine. Though both acknowledge that they are inexorably a part of one another, only Heathcliff is willing to face the consequences of that acknowledgment. Little by little, he brings Catherine to the point where she, too, can confess her love, but it is no accident that the terrible moment of her surrender to the truth coincides with the moment of her death.

Catherine dies before the book is half over, but her spirit continues to rage in the turbulent air of Wuthering Heights, haunting Heathcliff; her spirit returns, healthily subdued, in her daughter and her nephew Hareton.

MR. EARNSHAW

Mr. Earnshaw, Cathy and Hindley's father, appears only briefly at the beginning of the novel; nevertheless, he is an important character. It is he who brings the dark orphan Heathcliff from Liverpool to the Heights, and it is this act which starts the story on its inevitable way. Why was Earnshaw attracted to this particular child among many? Are we dealing here with a first manifestation of Heathcliff's magnetic power which later attracted Catherine and Isabella and Hareton to him and which made it possible for him to achieve success in the world in only three years? Perhaps; but in any event Mr. Earnshaw was willing to carry this boy on his back the many weary miles from Liverpool His only thanks on arriving home was the ill will of the entire household. Was the gesture wholly an altruistic one? Was Mr. Earnshaw really considering Heathcliff's welfare or his own? He had long been dissatisfied with his son, Hindley. Another son—named Heathcliff—had died. Is it possible that the second Heathcliff was meant to be a substitute for the first, to dispossess Hindley just as Hindley feared? It seems likely that for Mr. Earnshaw, Heathcliff was in large part a tool and that, therefore, the boy first learned the art of using people—an art he was later to bring to perfection—from his benefactor. But if Heathcliff was intended all along by Earnshaw to be an affront to the family, there was never a real chance for him to be anything else, and the tragedy is inescapable.

MRS. EARNSHAW

Mrs. Earnshaw is a minor character in the novel. In her favor it might be said that her annoyance with the intrusion into her family of the gypsy boy, Heathcliff, is perhaps healthier than her husband's suspect altruism.

HINDLEY EARNSHAW

Hindley Earnshaw, the at first vicious and later dissolute son of Mr. Earnshaw, is a character the reader can more readily understand than sympathize with. Dispossessed of his father's love, presumably by Heathcliff (though in reality much earlier), Hindley can quite literally do nothing but strike out at the usurper. *Wuthering Heights* is a novel about inheritances, inheritances of all sorts, and it begins with Hindley's failure to come into the legacy of his father's affection. We know that Heathcliff's revenge on Hindley is designed to pay the latter back for all the torment he inflicted on the young orphan. What we should also remember is that torment was in its turn a kind of revenge on Heathcliff for taking the eldest son's place in his father's heart. (Heathcliff, symbolically, was carried from Liverpool at the expense of the toys Earnshaw had promised to bring his children.) Both men were dispossessed, then, and both, being deprived of love, lost the ability to feel it. When we are most inclined to condemn Hindley we should remember that he is the father of the promising Hareton.

FRANCES

Frances is the wife Hindley brings home with him from college. She is a foolish, sickly girl who is at first delighted by everything she sees at the Heights, but whose shallow nature makes it impossible for her to respond to the real beauty of the world she has come to live in. She has hardly given birth to her son Hareton when she dies, leaving Hindley distracted and dissolute, an easy prey for the vengeful Heathcliff.

HARETON EARNSHAW

Hareton Earnshaw, the son of Hindley and Frances, turns out

to be more promising than the reader, knowing his parents, might expect. Though he is ground down by Heathcliff and deprived of every opportunity for enlightenment, he has a capacity for affection—affection even for his tormentor—that is his saving grace. With the help of young Catherine Linton, he struggles toward the achievement of his inheritance, a struggle which the exhausted Heathcliff no longer has the strength to oppose. On the day Hareton reads aloud his name, carved over the entrance of Wuthering Heights, we know that he cannot for long be kept from his legacy.

MR. AND MRS. LINTON

Mr. and Mrs. Linton appear only briefly in the novel. It is their fate to invite Catherine to convalesce with them after her childhood illness, to contract the illness themselves, and to die. There could be no better illustration of the way in which Catherine Earnshaw introduces the principle of stormy violence into the more civilized atmosphere.

EDGAR LINTON

Edgar Linton, to whom elegant Thrushcross Grange passes on the death of his parents, is himself mild, tenderhearted and cheerful, if also on occasion pettish and a snob. Very naturally, he appears weak and cold-blooded beside the violent Heathcliff, but he is described as the sort of pleasant, patient man most women would be happy to have for a husband. Spoiled and delicate as a child, he becomes, as he matures, a sturdy member of society, a magistrate, a gentle man who can be spirited when the occasion calls for it, and whose sense of responsibility extends beyond his own child to those of his sister and his brothers-in-law. If he makes a mistake, it is in marrying Catherine, a woman so different from him in every way, and so plainly a creature of the storm. Yet he loves her very much and, as his death approaches, he speaks of rejoining her with as much sincerity as Heathcliff, if with less violence. On the death of Catherine, he becomes a recluse, but is gradually drawn back to life by his daughter. At his death, he seems almost saintly, if still rather pallid.

CATHERINE LINTON

Catherine Linton is her father's darling. She combines Edgar's tender-heartedness with her mother's rebellious, high-spirited nature; thus, her character represents the possibility of a reconciliation between the Heights and the Grange. Her affectionate nature traps her into the marriage with Linton, but it is that same ability to give and receive love which attracts her at last to Hareton.

ISABELLA LINTON

Isabella Linton, the sister of Edgar and the mother of Linton Heathcliff, is a weak, flighty character. Where her brother is gentle and persistent, she is weak-willed and irresolute, and there can be no greater condemnation of her judgment or her powers of observation than her decision to marry Heathcliff. She must be credited with having had the strength to abandon her husband and take up a lonely life with her son near London. But her major characteristics remain those which she passes on to the young Linton.

LINTON HEATHCLIFF

Linton Heathcliff is a nervous, sickly child, weak-willed and petulant like his mother, and, like her, the pitiful victim and tool of his father. It is ironic that the robust, passionate Heathcliff should have had so sickly a son as Linton, but the symbolism is clear. Hate is barren. Only the worst traits of both parents have survived this loveless marriage—the peevishness and self-pity of the mother, and the bad temper of the father.

MR. LOCKWOOD

Mr. Lockwood is the tenant Heathcliff finds for the property he has stolen from Cathy. Lockwood is a city man, obviously gregarious and well-adapted to civilized life, who has taken it into his head, because of an unfortunate love affair, to play at being an antisocial misanthrope. He does not know what misanthropy means, however, until he encounters his landlord, Mr. Heathcliff; and in fact he is never really able to understand fully his strange, north-country neighbors. He makes some ludicrous mistakes of judgment in the course of the book—the most ludicrous being his idea that there might some day be something between himself and Cathy (an idea no reader can take seriously); but like the other narrators in the book, he is precise and honest in his reporting of what he sees. He gives the reader an opportunity to compare events as they happened with Lockwood's evaluation of them, and to note the ironic contrasts. One of Lockwood's chief functions is to remind the reader that there really are such places as London and Bath in a universe which also contains Wuthering Heights.

ELLEN DEAN, OR NELLY

Ellen Dean, or Nelly, is the sturdy housekeeper from whose lips we hear most of the story of *Wuthering Heights*. She works by turns at the Heights and the Grange and at one time or another is confided in by nearly all the major characters, so that there is ample justification for her apparent omniscience. Still, she seems so expert a storyteller that Emily Brontë feels called upon to comment on her skill by having Lockwood compliment the housekeeper on her unusual talent. As with Lockwood, however, precision of narrative in Nelly is not be equated with acuteness of judgment. In fact, one of the great tensions of the novel is the one which exists between Nelly's evaluation of events and the reader's. Nelly's comments on characters are nearly always shallow: she dismisses Heathcliff as evil, Catherine as flighty, and Edgar as infatuated—and at one point her insensitivity actually affects the course of the story, when she tells Edgar that his wife's illness is feigned, though in fact it is genuine. As one critic has suggested, Nelly's obtuseness is one of the most important instruments of the narrative, forcing the reader to participate directly in the story in order to discover its profoundest truths.

JOSEPH

Joseph, the old retainer at Wuthering Heights, is described by

Nelly as "the wearisomest, self-righteous Pharisee that ever ransacked a Bible to rake the promises to himself and fling the curses at his neighbors." Perhaps Nelly once more oversimplifies, for Joseph does not seem quite as malicious as this in the book. He is, of course, narrow-minded, bigoted and wholly committed to his hard religion. Yet the reader cannot help but feel that it is persistence in a dark, life-hating creed rather than an actual desire to give pain to others which best characterizes Joseph's nature. Indeed, it is even possible to feel sorry for the old man when he finds his black-currant trees dug up in Chapter 33 and speaks of being uprooted himself. Yet the removal of the trees does in fact symbolize the end of Joseph's influence at the Heights. The harshness and crabbedness of soul which he represents is replaced by the loving, accepting natures of Hareton and Catherine. Flowers from the Grange will grow where the black-currant trees once stood.

ZILLAH

Zillah, the housekeeper at the Heights during Nelly's stay at the Grange, narrates the events contained in Chapter 30 and is represented there as a cold, selfish woman who refuses to take action or even to speak out in a way that might save Linton's life, because she is a "good servant" and doesn't meddle in matters that are none of her business. The Zillah of Chapter 30 contrasts strangely with the Zillah of Chapter 2, a "lusty dame" who goes to the rescue of Lockwood when no one else will help him. It is often just as difficult for a novelist to achieve reasonable consistency in minor characters as in major ones.

MR. KENNETH

Mr. Kenneth is the neighborhood physician. In England, not all medical practitioners were permitted to call themselves "doctor."

MR. GREEN

Mr. Green is the local lawyer, an unscrupulous man who fails to appear in time to help the dying Edgar change his will because he has "sold himself" to Heathcliff.

MICHAEL AND OTHER MINOR CHARACTERS

Various characters such as the herd-boy, the milk-fetcher, etc., perform various minor functions in the plot without actually being in any way characterized themselves. Only Michael, the stable-boy, is given the briefest identity: the reader is informed that he is fond of reading.

CRITICAL COMMENTARY

EARLY YEARS

Together with Agnes Grey, *Wuthering Heights* was first published in December, 1847, by Thomas C. Newby. Newby was primarily a printer, though he did occasionally publish—that is to say, distribute and advertise—the books he printed, and he consented to handle Emily's and Anne's novels only if the Brontës would share the risk of the venture by paying him 50 pounds in advance.

The women performed their share of the bargain, but Newby was somewhat less than conscientious about performing his. He had undertaken to print 350 copies of the works and in fact only printed 250; he was slow in sending proof sheets to the authors; and to a great extent, he ignored the corrections made in proof by Emily and Anne. Thus the books were full of errors, and after Emily's death in 1848, Charlotte labored to correct the mistakes for the second edition of *Wuthering Heights*, brought out in December, 1850.

During these early years of the novel's existence, a number of critical commentaries appeared in the press and elsewhere, including Charlotte's own preface to the new edition. Though tradition has it that Emily's genius went unrecognized by the critics of her own time, many of the reviews were in fact quite sensible and even enthusiastic.

UNFAVORABLE REACTION

There were, of course, the usual number of unperceptive comments. *Wuthering Heights* was not the sort of book to appeal to critics with rigid notions about what novels ought to be. H. F. Chorley, in the December 25, 1847 issue of the *Athenaeum*, dismissed the work as a "disagreeable story," appearing at a time when England needed "sunshine more than ever." The *Quarterly Review* waited a whole year to acknowledge the existence of the book, and then said of it that "with all the unscrupulousness of the French school of novels it combines that repulsive vulgarity in the choice of its vice which supplies its own antidote." The critic went even further out on a limb, saying that the book could not have been written by a woman, or if it had been, then only by a woman who had "long forfeited the society of her own sex." Still other foolish remarks are on record. *The Spectator* found the novel's "incidents and persons . . . too coarse and disagreeable to be attractive," while the *North American Review* saw in the book an "attempt to corrupt the virtue of the sturdy descendants of the Puritans."

ENCOURAGING RESPONSE

At the same time, there was a good deal of generous and understanding commentary about the book. Charlotte Brontë's own favorite review (it may have been her favorite because the reviewer, Sydney Dobell, under the impression that the book's author was really Charlotte, took the occasion to praise *Wuthering Heights* very warmly) appeared in the *Palladium* in September, 1850. "Let the critic take up the book;" writes Dobell, "lay it down in what thought he will, there are some things in it he can lay down no more." He then goes on to praise, with special enthusiasm, the characters of Catherine Earnshaw, Nelly Dean, and Joseph. To be sure, Dobell speaks of the work as "the unformed writing of a giant's hand: the 'large utterance' of a baby god." But he concludes his remarks by repeating that "there are passages in this book of '*Wuthering Heights*' of which any novelist, past or present, might be proud," and praises particularly the account of Lockwood's second visit to the Heights.

Other reviewers were equally impressed with the "strange originality" and the "considerable power" of the book, and while none could refrain from offering some adverse criticism of its wildness, even Charlotte Brontë was forced to acknowledge, in her preface to the 1850 edition, that to readers unacquainted with Yorkshire, *Wuthering Heights* "must appear a rude and strange production."

In a way, the first reviewers of great works of art have the most difficult critical job to perform, for they must not only say what the book is about, they must also say whether it is good or bad. Later critics do not, of course, have to evaluate the work. They begin with the assumption that it is great, and, secure on this point, are free to make careful analyses of it and explore all its meanings. This is what the later critics of *Wuthering Heights* have done.

In 1926 C. P. Sanger published an essay entitled "The Structure of *Wuthering Heights*" which includes a chapter-by-chapter timetable of the events in the novel, as well as the genealogical table which appears early in this book. What Sanger is most impressed with is the precision with which Emily Brontë handled the many details of her novel. Characters are always the ages they are supposed to be in every chapter and are always acting their age. The geography of the area is always given scrupulous accuracy, and even so specialized a subject as the English inheritance law is handled with accuracy. The great value of Sanger's study in its day was dispel any idea that *Wuthering Heights* was structurally wild or disorganized, as many early critics had found it to be, and to permit other readers to penetrate to the real source of the book's violent, chaotic energy.

LATER CRITICISM

In recent years the field of literary studies has changed tremendously. Movements such as feminism, psychoanalysis, cultural studies, and post-colonialist studies have opened up the way we read English literature. Over the last few decades scholars have waged a fierce debate concerning the "canon" of English literature. This debate was fueled, in part, by a desire to reach out to many different kinds of students. *Wuthering Heights* holds an important place in this debate. Written by a woman, it is clearly an indisputable "masterpiece" and it has found its way onto many required reading lists. Of course, some scholars have argued that, because there were few women writers prior to the 20th Century, it is logical that such reading lists will include primarily male authors. Emily Brontë sometimes appears as the "token woman" and this has prompted scholars to ask if there is something specifically "feminine" about the way she writes. The romantic aspect of Heathcliff's character has been pointed out by scholars as representative of a type of female fantasy, while other scholars have argued that Brontë writes rich prose that should not be considered either male or female.

ESSAY QUESTIONS AND ANSWERS

Question

What is the symbolic significance of Wuthering Heights and Thrushcross Grange in the novel?

Answer

A number of critics have suggested that these two houses embody the two major principles of life in the book: storm and calm. Wuthering Heights is located on a hill and is constantly buffeted by wild winds. The trees have been stunted by these winds, and the house itself has survived the constant battering only because of its massive, rugged construction. The inhabitants of the Heights also seem creatures of the storm. They are constantly being torn by strong passions, and violence is their natural language. They are farmers; they work the land and their reactions to life are elemental.

In contrast, Thrushcross Grange is set in a well-landscaped park, comparatively sheltered from the wild elements. The style of the house and its furnishings are much more delicate and refined than those of the Heights. The Lintons are not farmers but country squires. They have tenants and have the political and social obligations of the landed gentry. The people of the Grange are gentle and seek not so much the wild sparkle and dance of life as its repose.

It is very important that the terms "calm" and "storm" not be equated with the ideas of "good" and "evil." Nowhere in her novel does Emily Brontë suggest that the inhabitants of the Heights are all bad or that the people who live at the Grange are all good. Heathcliff and Catherine may be wild and destructive but they are also capable of great sensitivity and love. And Edgar may be gentle and responsible, but he is also snobbish and cold. "Calm" and "storm," then, represent the two poles of existence, not value judgments of it. And when elements from each end of the scale find themselves thrust to the other end, the resulting violence and conflict can only be resolved by discovering a mid-point between the two extremes. When the children of the two houses, Hareton and Cathy, meet and marry, such a resolution is achieved in *Wuthering Heights*.

Question

What is Heathcliff's place in the history of English literature?

Answer

Every great artist creates characters who are unique, who are incomparably themselves, who have never existed before and who will never exist again. Heathcliff is such a character. Search everywhere in English literature and you will never find another Heathcliff. You will, however, find certain characters who resemble Heathcliff to a greater or lesser extent.

Emily Brontë wrote her novel in the late 1840s, some years after the high point of the English Romantic Movement. The great Romantics, among them Blake, Wordsworth, Coleridge, Keats, Shelley, and Byron, emphasized in their writing the inner reality of the human spirit. And as they delved deeper and deeper into his internal nature they found not only sources of nobility and dignity, but also certain stubborn elements of darkness and violence which seemed to form an integral and ineradicable part of being. It was only one step from this discovery to the development, in Romantic literature, of the so-called Satanic hero who had great qualities of mind and heart but who was also, quite obviously, a product of that inner darkness.

It was largely the Romantic Movement which elevated Satan, the villain of John Milton's *Paradise Lost*, to the level of hero, seeing in his rebelliousness a metaphor for our constant striving for individual freedom, of which the French Revolution of 1789 was considered another metaphor. New characters were created on this satanic model. Byron's dark hero Manfred is a good example, as are Shelley's Prometheus, the great rebel against God, and Herman Melville's Captain Ahab from the novel *Moby-Dick*. Heathcliff is worthy of this company. He is himself like a fallen angel, a person of great magnetism and potential who has been overwhelmed by the elements of darkness, and he is clearly a character designed for readers who are willing to acknowledge the darkness in themselves.

Question

Comment on the structure of *Wuthering Heights*.

Answer

Early critics of the novel were often confused by the arrangement of events and called the structure of the work irrational. Actually, however, the departures from chronology are essential to the telling of the story. What Emily Brontë hoped to do in her book was to reveal, very gradually, the truth about a remarkable human relationship. She wanted to give her readers an opportunity to circle in slowly toward the center of that truth, and so she undertook to show them first the chronological extremes of the action and then to let these converge on the center. Our interest is first aroused in the strange, violent family at Wuthering Heights in the last days of its agony. We are then shown that family at the beginning of its career; and at last we arrive, from two directions at once, it seems, at the center of the story, the great love of Heathcliff and Catherine.

Given this sort of chronology, the use of multiple narrators is almost inevitable. When a book is written from the point of view of the so-called omniscient author, a god-like creature who hovers in the air over the world, able to see past, present, and future in the same instant, there can be no excuse for toying with the natural order of events. Such an author would be accused of playing tricks, of being unfair to the reader. When a number of narrators, all with different experiences, tell a story, however, chronological distortion is almost inevitable and so can be justified.

When Emily Brontë used the multiple narrator technique, though, she made it pay a special dividend. By creating, in her narrators, not simply mouthpieces for the author, but real people, capable of making mistakes of judgment, she was able to draw her readers intimately into her story. For where there is a discrepancy between what the narrator says has happened, and what the reader can see has happened, the reader's judgment becomes essential for an understanding of the book. Mr. Lockwood makes certain remarks about his interest in young Catherine Linton which only the alert reader can appreciate the absurdity of, and at least part of our sympathy for Heathcliff stems from our desire to counteract some of the harsher judgments of the boy offered by Nelly Dean.

BIBLIOGRAPHY

BIOGRAPHIES

Chitham, Edward. *A Life of Emily Brontë.* New York: Basil Blackwell, 1987.

Frank, Katherine. *A Chainless Soul: A Life of Emily Brontë.* Boston: Houghton Mifflin, 1990.

Knapp, Bettina. *The Brontës: Branwell, Anne, Emily, Charlotte.* New York: Continuum, 1991.

CRITICAL BOOKS

Benvenuto, Richard. *Emily Brontë.* Boston: Twayne, 1982.

Bloom, Harold, ed. *Emily Brontë's* Wuthering Heights. New York: Chelsea House, 1987.

Bloom, Harold, ed. *Heathcliff.* New York: Chelsea House, 1993.

Brontë, Emily; Peterson, Linda H., ed. Wuthering Heights: *Complete, Authoritative Text with Bibliographical and Historical Contexts, Critical History, and Essays from Five Contemporary Critical Perspectives.* Boston: Bedford Books of St. Martin's press, 1992.

Caine, Jeffrey. *Heathcliff.* New York: Knopf, 1978.

Davies, Stevie. *Emily Brontë.* Bloomington: Indiana University Press, 1988.

Kavanagh, James H. *Emily Brontë.* New York: Basil Blackwell, 1985.

Knoepflmacher, U. C. Wuthering Heights*: A Study.* Athens: Ohio University Press, 1994.

Miles, Peter. *Wuthering Heights.* Basingstoke: Macmillan Education, 1990.

ARTICLES

Dawson, Terence, "The Struggle for Deliverance from the Father: The Structural Principle of *Wuthering Heights,*" *Modern Language Review* 84 (1989), 289–304.

Farrell, John P., "Reading the Text of Community in *Wuthering Heights,*" *ELH* 56 (1989), 173–208.

Goff, Barbara Munson, "Between Natural Theology and Natural Selection: Breeding the Human Animal in *Wuthering Heights,*" *Victorian Studies* 27 (1983–1984), 477–508.

Haggerty, George E., "The Gothic Form of *Wuthering Heights,*" *Victorian Newsletter* No. 74 (Fall 1988), 1–6.

Landon, Bette, "*Wuthering Heights* and the Text between the Lines," *Papers on Language and Literature* 24 (1988), 34–52.

McGuire, Kathryn B., "The Incest Taboo in *Wuthering Heights*: A Modern Appraisal," *American Imago* 45 (1988), 217–224.

Macovski, Michael S., "*Wuthering Heights* and the Rhetoric of Interpretation," *ELH* 54 (1987), 363–384.

Newman, Beth, "'The Situation of the Looker-On': Gender, Narration, and Gaze in *Wuthering Heights,*" *PMLA* 105 (1990), 1029–1041.

Oates, Joyce Carol, "The Magnamity of *Wuthering Heights,*" *Critical Inquiry* 9 (1982), 35–49.

Sanger, C. P, "The Structure of *Wuthering Heights,*" in Wuthering Heights: *Authoritative Text, Backgrounds, Criticism/Emily Brontë*, eds., William M. Sale and Richard J. Dunn. New York: Norton, 1990.

Senf, Carol A., "Emily Brontë's Version of Feminist History: *Wuthering Heights*," *Essays in Literature* 12 (1985), 201–214.

Stevenson, W. H., "*Wuthering Heights*: The Facts," *Essays in Criticism* 35 (1985), 146–166.

Williams, Anne, "Natural Supernaturalism in *Wuthering Heights*," *Studies in Philology* 82 (1985), 104–127.

NOTES